LC AAM

Europeanization, European Integration and Financial Services

Europeanization, European Integration and Financial Services

Developing Theoretical Frameworks and Synthesising Methodological Approaches

Kerry E. Howell

First published 2004 by
PALGRAVE MACMILLAN
Houndmills, Basingstoke, Hampshire RG21 6XS and
175 Fifth Avenue, New York, N.Y. 10010
Companies and representatives throughout the world

PALGRAVE MACMILLAN is the global academic imprint of the Palgrave Macmillan division of St. Martin's Press, LLC and of Palgrave Macmillan Ltd. Macmillan® is a registered trademark in the United States, United Kingdom and other countries. Palgrave is a registered trademark in the European Union and other countries.

ISBN 1–4039–1255–6

This book is printed on paper suitable for recycling and made from fully managed and sustained forest sources.

A catalogue record for this book is available from the British Library.

Library of Congress Cataloging-in-Publication Data
Howell, Kerry E.
    Europeanization, European integration and financial services :
    developing theoretical frameworks and synthesising methodological
    approaches / Kerry E. Howell.
        p. cm.
    Includes bibliographical references and index.
    ISBN 1–4039–1255–6 (cloth)
    1. Europe – Economic integration. 2. European Union. 3. Financial
    services industry – Government policy – European Union countries.
    I. Title.

HC241.H693 2004
337.1'42—dc22   2003070076

10 9 8 7 6 5 4 3 2 1
13 12 11 10 09 08 07 06 05 04

Printed and bound in Great Britain by
Antony Rowe Ltd, Chippenham and Eastbourne

For my Mother and in memory of my late Father (1940–92)

Contents

Preface and Acknowledgements

The rationale for this study emerged through discussions with colleagues on a University Association for Contemporary European Studies (UACES) and Economic and Social Research Council (ESRC) project entitled the Europeanization of British Politics and Public Policy at Sheffield University. This project began in 2001 and was led by Stephen George and Ian Bache and involved a number of extremely informative discussions with David Allen, Jim Buller, Simon Bulmer, Martin Burch, Michelle Cini, Jenny Fairbrass, Andrew Gamble, Robert Geyer, Ricardo Gomez, Erin van der Maas, Jill Preston and Nigel Waddington.

Discussions were based around theoretical conceptualizations of Europeanization and the differences between Europeanization and European integration. The discussions also attempted to clarify how the project would use the concept of Europeanization and how this may best serve an analysis of British politics and public policy. Methodological perspectives and theoretical frameworks regarding Europeanization were also considered at the UACES conference, Newcastle University 2003, Public Administration Conference, York University 2002, the Department of Politics Seminar Series, York University 2003 and School of Finance and Law, Financial Services Seminar Series, Bournemouth University 2003. I would like to thank Ian Bache, Stephen George, Philip Hardwick and Stuart Wall for useful comments on earlier drafts of particular chapters.

A clear illustration of Europeanization could be realized through concentrating on downloading which would in many cases clearly identify cause and effect. However, if this approach is used then numerous variables in terms of uploading and crossloading are lost and a thin explanation rather than thick understanding will be the outcome of research and analysis. These issues are taken up in this text and in some instances conclusions are tentatively made.

In such a way, this text is primarily concerned with developing methodological approaches and theoretical frameworks to provide explanations and understanding regarding Europeanization, European integration and the European Union (EU). This area of study is continually changing and as I write, Enlargement is taking place and a European constitution being formulated through intergovernmental conferences and European integration. The EU is a strange beast and means divergent things to different people (Puchala, 1972) and given that we are unsure of what we have at the outset of the analysis, prediction is extremely difficult. Consequently, research in the area of European integration often begins with an examination of what the EU is, rather than what it should become. That is not to say normative analysis does not exist because in many instances, defining the EU, automatically calls into question the direction it should take.

KERRY E. HOWELL

About the Author

Dr Howell is currently a Reader in Governance, Director of the Research Centre for Institutional Governance and Jean Monnet Teaching Fellow in the Ashcroft International Business School at APU. His other responsibilities include, Joint Director of the Doctorate in Business Administration Programme, Chair of the Business School Research Degrees Committee, Committee Member of the University Association of Contemporary European Studies and membership of a number of editorial boards.

Working in academia for over a decade, Dr Howell has been an Association of British Insurers PhD candidate and worked as a research fellow and senior lecturer. He has also acted as a senior research fellow for Frizzell Insurance (now Liverpool Victoria), as a political adviser for political lobbyists in Brussels and as a consultant for economic forecasters as well as numerous companies and interest groups. He was awarded a PhD in political science and has since published widely in academic journals and written a number of books/monographs on European integration and financial services, the Eurozone and Europeanization.

General Introduction: Linking Levels of Theory and Methodological Approaches

Introduction

This book investigates the role of theory in an understanding and explanation of European integration and Europeanization. Through a historical study of European integration, treaty developments and studies of Europeanization in terms of financial services this text illustrates different levels of theory in relation to cause and effect, verification, reliability, generalization and prediction. In the social sciences it is generally accepted that positivist prediction is difficult to achieve and with this in mind they should pursue controlled generalization or idealized prediction.

This study identifies four levels of abstraction in the form of political philosophy, grand theory, meso theory and substantive theory respectively, with each level providing insight into European integration processes at different levels of activity. This study is not primarily concerned with prediction but uses levels of theory to explain and understand European integration and Europeanization. As noted in Popper (1994). 'The future is open. It is not predetermined and thus cannot be predicted ... the possibilities that lie in the future are infinite' (p. xiii). However, outcomes depend on humanity, we are responsible for our own future. 'It is our duty to remain optimists, this includes not only the openness of the future but also that which all of us contribute to it by everything we do: we are all responsible for what the future holds in store. Thus it is our duty, not to prophesise evil but, rather, to fight for a better world' (ibid.).

1

Dahrendorf (2003) considered that the European Union (EU) was about the development of a 'lawful liberal order' and that in Kantian terms, antagonisms are the source of progress.

> In the end, such progress might envisage an international order of lively competition and conflict under the law. We have a long way to go to such an order; perhaps we shall never reach it. In the meantime, however, we must act in such a way that the maxims of our actions can be thought of as the principles of a cosmopolitan order. (p. 23)

In this context, the EU is not simply about unification it is also about nurturing diversity. Under a civil constitution of liberty (as a basis of western or liberal values) EU member states adjust their own cultural traditions. These are not wholesale changes (because such values are applicable in most parts of the world) but changes that bring them into line with the main tenets of the civil constitution. Dahrendorf (2003) cited the rule of law as an example, but points out that the values embedded in this are more than European.

> They are western, uniting Europe, the United States and important countries in other parts of the world. As the way the Organisation for Economic Co-operation and Development has become the most plausible representation of the values in question ... would it be an idea to set up an OPCD, an Organisation for Political Co-operation and development to help to spread and guard the constitution across the world? (ibid.)

However, Kagan (2003) identified the main differences between the United States and the EU in terms of their political philosophies. Because of the change in the balance of power he argued that, 'Europeans have stepped out of the Hobbesian world of anarchy into the Kantian world of perpetual peace' (p. 59). Indeed, the EU has rejected military power and replaced confrontation with co-operation and integration. The EU is a postmodern structure in that it does not rely on balance of power politics but on the rejection of force (Cooper, 2003; Kagan, 2003). It has moved away from realist ideas of power politics and taken up idealist notions relating to functionalism and neo-functionalism. There are also philosophical and theoretical perspectives outlined in Dahrendorf (2003), regarding neo functionalism and functionalism, in relation to a civil constitution and Europeanization in the form of value adjustments, recognition and diversity. Political philosophy and grand theories organize concepts and enable humanity to identify desired ends in an open future; whereas meso theories, such as Europeanization, and elements of this in the form of substantive theory, attempt to enable verifiable generalizations and empirical reliability, but at the cost of deeper understandings of process in terms of interaction and continuity. Overall, 'theories are nets cast to catch what we call the world: to rationalize to explain and to master it. We endeavour to make the mesh ever finer' (Popper, 2002, p. 38).

This study synthesizes a number of areas relating to European integration, Europeanization and financial services in both theoretical and empirical terms. Financial services are central to the process of European integration and will continue to be so as the EU and the Single European Market (SEM) develop. In this sense financial services enable clarification of the theoretical perspectives of European integration. At the same time changes in the domestic and EU financial services sectors can be understood in more depth and greater detail through the utilization of these theories; in this context and for this text the relationship between theory and practice is iterative and interactive.

This text bases its understanding of theory on different paradigms used in understanding the form of reality and what can be known about it (ontology), the relationship between the investigator and what can be discovered (epistemology) and the framework the investigator may use in the discovery process (methodology).

Positivism, identified during the mid-nineteenth century and closely linked with empiricism and naturalism was an attempt by the social sciences to mimic the methodological approaches outlined for the natural sciences. It was developed by Comte and Saint-Simon and argued that human thought evolved through three stages; the religious, metaphysic and scientific. However, even though the later stage exemplified the highest form of thought, the earlier stages had their value and were not to be discarded as primitive or useless. Positivism was both descriptive and normative; it described how human thought had evolved and prescribed norms for how it should develop. It had an axiological perspective, which argued that human duty was to further the process that existed, though positivism was more concerned with methodological approaches than prescribing ethical norms. However, there was an emphasis on identifying and determining the inevitable, a trait shared with Marxism. Comte's hierarchy put human science at the top, which precipitated and emphasized the science of humanity or sociology. It was becoming clear that people (at least as masses) were suitable phenomenon for scientific study, a realization which led to humanity being studied in institutions which were developing themselves. Following Comte there was less emphasis on the categorization of human development; the emphasis on the centrality and all embracing perspective of science remained but metaphysics and religion were peripherized and denied. Positivism became a critical approach to science itself; to what science was and what it could achieve. Science should be based on observation alone, and no appeal should be made to what cannot be observed. There should be no recourse to metaphysical debate, all should be simplified and prediction pursued.

The problem with positivism was that it omitted and alienated many approaches to generating understanding, knowledge and theory and was eventually challenged by post-positivism. Ontologically, positivism considered that an external reality existed, which could be discovered and totally understood, an approach sometimes labelled 'naïve realism'. If the investigator and the external world (or what could be discovered) were totally separate and objectivity sought through scientific procedure, truth could be found (epistemology). Indeed, this could be achieved by testing and attempting to prove hypotheses, through scientific experiments and the manipulation of confounding conditions (methodology). This paradigm allows a distinct understanding of theory in that theory provides set immutable laws, which enable prediction. Immutable laws and prediction are difficult enough in the natural sciences, but in the social sciences, in most instances, almost impossible. This was one of the major criticisms levelled at positivism by post-positivists who argued that reality or truth existed, however it could only be understood imperfectly or probabilistically.

Ontologically, post-positivism perceived reality as external to humanity but considered our intellectual capabilities unable to fully understand it. This has been identified as 'critical realism'. Epistemologically, post-positivism abandons the total separation between the investigated and investigator however objectivity and separation are still pursued. This leads to a methodology that deals with multiple modified scientific experimentation and hypothesis falsification. Theory is not about the discovery of immutable laws but the discovery of approximations to the truth. A new theory may deal with some difficulties but will invariably open many new problems. Indeed, if the theory provides significant progress then 'the new problems will differ from the old problems: the new problems will be on a radically different level of depth' (Popper, 1994, p. 4). Theory development is open to criticism. Consequently, through falsification 'we can get rid of a badly fitting theory' before it overrides investigation and undermines objectivity (ibid.).

This perspective still left problems for those social sciences, who sought to identify and challenge what was taking place in institutions from historical and mainly qualitative perspectives. This led to a criticism of post-positivism and the emergence of the critical theory paradigm (Guba and Lincoln, 1994). The critical theory paradigm included theoretical perspectives that challenged the status quo for example, neo-Marxism, feminism, determinism and so on, and provided a specific understanding of reality in that it was shaped by 'social, political, cultural, economic and gender values crystalised over time' (ibid., p. 105). A general perspective of critical theory ontology involves an understanding that reality is shaped through historical processes and may be defined as 'historical realism'. An example of this would be the nation-state in terms of its changing role within international relations and the issues this raised for ideas such as sovereignty and democratic accountability. As the role of the nation-state changes, so does our understanding of it, which has implications for our interpretation of reality in terms of the role of the state, the nation and sovereignty. Indeed, the EU and international institutions have implications for changes regarding these issues and provide the impetus for theoretical change as well as empirical outcomes.

The epistemological aspect of the critical theory paradigm considered that findings and theoretical perspectives are discovered because the investigator and investigated are intrinsically linked through historical values, which must influence the inquiry. This leads towards a specific methodology, which identifies a dialogic and dialectical approach. Dialogue is needed between the researcher and the researched and between past and present. In this methodology, structures are changeable and actions affect change. In this context, theory is changeable in relation to historical circumstance. Theory is developed by human beings in historical and cultural circumstances as the interaction between researcher and researched and historical values influence the analysis. Theory is not defined from a positivist perspective where immutable laws predict either forever or until they are displaced, but developed in a historical context: theory is developed by subjective humans in a historical context.

The fourth paradigm, dealt with in this text, namely constructivism, understands reality as locally constructed and based on shared experiences, even though groups/individuals are changeable; ontologically, this identifies a 'relativist realism'. Epistemologically, constructivism is similar to critical theory except that it considers that findings are created and develop as the investigation progresses. This means that results are created through consensus and individual constructions, including the constructions of the investigator. Theory in this paradigm is relative and changeable, reliability and prediction almost impossible and cause and effect difficult to identify.

This study attempts to mix separate ontologies, epistemologies and methodologies in its understanding of theory in an identification of the role theory plays in understanding and explaining the EU. Positivism is extreme in its interpretation of ontology and epistemology and is difficult to deal with in the social sciences, which causes a number of problems when attempting to mix positivist interpretations of theory with other paradigms. For instance if there is one totally understandable reality that may be discovered through immutable laws this contradicts the ontological positions of the other paradigms. It is not possible for naïve realism to coexist with the other ontologies, which makes synthesis impracticable. However, with the change in ontology and epistemology between positivism and postpositivism we observe the recognition of human fallibility and theory replacement through critical analysis. This accepts that theory changes through falsification, which in itself is part of a historical process; critical theory through challenging the status quo, renders this same point explicit. Consequently, although ontologies, epistemologies and methodological approaches initially seem exclusive, when we examine them in more detail they may be considered inclusive and provide the opportunity for mixing theoretical perspectives and methodological approaches to attain both explanation and understanding of phenomenon. Furthermore, these gradients of theory identify levels of normativism; for instance positivism would try and deny normative perspectives whereas constructivism would embrace them.

In the following discussions, for the sake of clarity the above paradigms will be labelled in a general sense, as positivist and constructivist, the former includes and primarily incorporates the above definition of post-positivism, the latter includes critical theory. This study understands the former as leaning towards modernism and the latter post-modernism. In the former, theory has to be objective, identify cause and effect, provide generalization or prediction and ensure reliability. The latter however, is more concerned with frameworks for providing insight, understanding and validity in historical and specific circumstances.

As regards these different interpretations of theory the text constructs a typology in relation to levels of theory. Broad philosophical perspectives and grand theory are not able to fit well with the positivist interpretation of theory even though grand theory would correspond more easily with post-positivism. On the other hand, although meso theory could also correspond with elements of constructivism it does provide a means by which post-positivist stipulations regarding theory could be realized. In this study we examine two philosophical perspectives namely those of Kant and Hegel, assess grand theories through functionalism, realism, neo-functionalism and intergovernmentalism and meso theories in terms of multilevel governance and Europeanization. Furthermore, through breaking down Europeanization we eventually identify substantive theory. Substantive theory is derived from one specific area or part of the research and can be identified by breaking down theory into constituent parts. Philosophical frameworks, grand and meso theories are incrementally more abstract and consequently conceptually advanced.

The more specific the level of theory, the easier it is to identify cause and effect or dependent and independent variables. However, the more specific the level the more difficult it is to provide full understanding and explanation. A mix between aspects of the substantive, meso and grand theories provides insight and understanding with some identification of cause and effect. However, grand theory and philosophical frameworks provide understanding with cause and effect, prediction or historical determinism negated. In dealing with the application of these philosophical frameworks and theories the text is broken down into three parts.

Part I deals with the philosophical underpinnings of European integration theories and Europeanization. Part II concentrates on historical processes and treaties, the Single European Market (SEM), Economic and Monetary Union (EMU), and sub-national, national and supranational institutions. Finally, Part III investigates member states regarding Europeanization and European integration processes and, through case studies, the impact on domestic financial services.

Part I

Chapter 1 deals with political philosophies that underpin theories of European integration and Europeanization. It illustrates how Kantian and Hegelian political philosophy can further our understanding of the EU, European integration and Europeanization. In an understanding of European integration and Europeanization it is worth noting the philosophical issues and theories that generated and informed them. With the SEM, EMU and Enlargement, both actual and potential members have given up certain freedoms or pooled sovereignty to be part of the EU. Indeed, this chapter argues that the reason states are prepared to do this can be explained through the Kantian 'civil constitution' and Hegelian 'recognition'. This text identifies this influence through dealing with each thinker in turn, then illustrates how their individual political philosophies may provide further understanding and explanation of European integration and the EU. The following chapter investigates theoretical perspectives in more detail and Parts II and III explain the historical process and identify empirical examples of 'civil constitutions' and 'recognition'.

Chapter 2 builds on the philosophical underpinnings identified in Chapter 1 and investigates grand theoretical perspectives relating to European integration that include realism and intergovernmentalism, functionalism and neo-functionalism. Chapter 2 then overviews what may be considered meso theories in terms of multilevel governance and state-centricism. However, the chapter also recognizes that these are criticized as theories and in some quarters perceived as descriptions. This study considers that this may be the case and through a mix of Europeanization and grand theories these meso perspectives, especially multilevel governance, permit reliable answers to be realized.

The realist and intergovernmental critique emphasizes the importance of the nation-state in the process of international relations and European integration, respectively. The realist model is based on an interpretation of Hegelian thought that is linked to a Hobbesian perspective of international relations. Realism is based on the concept of power and the motives of nation-states. Functionalism is the means by which change towards a goal of international collaboration is brought about; it is illustrated through organizations which would be designated specific tasks that would evolve as functional needs changed. The system incorporates the premise of peaceful co-operation. In Kantian terms, it pursues the concept of 'perpetual peace'. Unlike functionalism, neo-functionalism posits that integration is more easily realized in a regional setting. Functionalists conceded that a supranational state would keep peace at the regional level. However, it would also create a power bloc and would not ensure peace at the international level. Neo-functionalism argued that, through closer European integration, political parties and interest groups would accept that action needed to be taken at the supranational level. Interest groups and political parties would organize and function beyond the nation-state and define their interests in the new environment. Indeed, through these interactions they would sow the seeds of further agreements, which would eventually overtake those based at the national level. The parties involved adhere to the rule of law and, when confrontation existed, dissatisfactions would be channelled through legal avenues rather than aggression. Fundamentally, European integration progresses incrementally through extensions in supranationality, sub-national interests and spillover. Other perspectives have linked neo-functionalism (through supranational actors and interest groups) to multilevel governance and intergovernmentalism to state-centric governance. They concluded that the state-centric approach is not capable of fully explaining European policy-making processes; that EU decision-making and policy-making are of a multilevel nature.

Overall, there is now some agreement that a range of theories can be used to explain the realities, dynamics and complexities of European integration. Indeed, the amalgamation of ideas came about following the Single European Act (SEA), Qualified Majority Voting (QMV) and member state uncertainty about where the reassertion of the SEM would lead them. With the renewed emphasis on integration many realized that the EU was in the process of metamorphosis and that this would have major implications for actors, processes and outcomes of policy-making at all levels in Europe: supranational, national and sub-national. This research implies that there is an amalgamation of international relations approaches to European integration processes in the form of multilevel governance through a process of Europeanization that provides meso theory and substantive theory that are capable of mixing methodological approaches which widen our understanding of European integration processes.

Chapter 3 deals with distinct elements of Europeanization and the links between these and European integration. There are criticisms of Europeanization in terms of its similarity with European integration and that it is a new and fashionable term with many different definitions. Sometimes the concept is used narrowly to refer to the implementation of EU legislation at the domestic level and at other times more broadly to encapsulate areas like policy transfer and learning within the EU. 'It is sometimes used to identify the shift of national policy paradigms and instruments to the EU level. Other times ... it includes discourse and identities as well as structures and policies at the domestic level' (Dyson and Goetz, 2002, p. 2). Furthermore, Europeanization is also used to identify European integration as an independent variable and change in domestic systems or Europeanization as the dependent variable.

This text constructs a conceptualization of Europeanization based on downloading, uploading and crossloading and identifies an interaction between these and European integration as both 'situation' and 'process'. Uploading involves the use of national and subnational actors in the formulation of EU policy; downloading incorporates the means by which these policies are implemented at the domestic level. Crossloading identifies different perspectives of policy transfer and the role of this in European integration. The distinction between Europeanization and European integration is also made explicit. Differences exist between Europeanization and European integration although they do continuously interact; for instance the development of the supranational level in the context of evolving institutions can be seen as European integration. Uploading indicates the use of governments or sub-national interests in the development of European integration and the switch towards a new centre of policy-making.

In this way, uploading can either be seen on a macro level, where governments formulate grand transformations in terms of the SEA, the SEM, EMU and Financial Services Action Plan (FSAP). Or it can be seen on a micro level, where other interests involve themselves in the process through interest groupings and networks. Governments outline their intention to compromise their positions in formulating macro decisions, however (especially in relation to the SEM) sub-national, national and EU actors work out the detail of compromise in the realization of regulatory structures. Consequently, the conceptualization of Europeanization, forwarded in this text, perceives institutional linkages in terms of governmental activity, interest group intermediation and network interaction and identifies these as the means by which preferences are uploaded to the EU and impact on the development of political structures and EU legislation. Conversely, examples of European integration incorporate the actual transformation of both the EU political structure (changing political space) and legislation (evolving directives, regulations etc.).

Part II

Part Two provides a historical overview of the EU and through the treaties identifies and analyses examples of issues raised through the philosophical perspectives and theoretical frameworks in Part I. For instance, the basis of Kant's 'civil constitution' is 'perpetual peace' and one may posit that the basis of the EU is peaceful coexistence and economic interaction based on the recognition of democracy and capitalism (even though different models of these exist throughout the membership). Consequently, Part II outlines historical process in relation to expectations and ideals involved in the foundations and evolution of the EU.

Chapter 4 covers the historical experience of Europe during the twentieth century and the ideals of the founders of the EU. For example in the European Coal and Steel Community (ECSC), Jean Monnet and Robert Schuman perceived a peaceful coexistence and economic regeneration in post-Second World War Europe. In more explicit (and functionalist) terms these sentiments can be observed in treaties where it was envisaged that European unity could be achieved through the creation of specialized administrative bodies at the European level which, by carrying out specific functions, would attract political authority to themselves. Such can be observed in the attempt to underpin Franco-German reconciliation through pooling the production of two strategically important industries, coal and steel. The Treaty of Paris (that initiated the ECSC) involved both political and economic objectives; peaceful coexistence and economic regeneration. Consequently, through a historical study of the EU, this chapter deals with the ongoing treaties that have been functionally developed by the EU and member states in the intensification of European integration and how these treaties provide the basis for Europeanization.

Jean Monnet and Robert Schuman perceived long-term political objectives in the gradual evolution of the EU from economic integration to political union. Indeed, this premise could be seen as the basis of a number of treaties that followed the Treaty of Paris including the Treaty of Rome, the SEA, the Maastricht Treaty, the Treaty of Amsterdam and Nice. Chapter 5 deals with each of the treaties and their practical ramifications and relate these to European integration and Europeanization processes. Furthermore, Chapter 5 explains the history of the SEM in terms of the SEA and the Maastricht Treaty and indicates how the project has relied on the harmonization and re-regulation of the financial services sector. Chapter 5 also examines EMU and the Treaty of Maastricht in more detail as well as the Werner report and Delors plan, and the realization of the single currency. The chapter draws on theoretical perspectives and identifies issues linked with Europeanization through an investigation of policy impacts on domestic structures.

Two rival schools relating to EMU had emerged by the late 1960s. The monetarists wanted exchange rates fixed immediately while the economists wanted co-ordination and harmonization prior to fixed exchange rates. Eventually, a compromise between the two schools was realized in the Delors plan and the subsequent timetable outlined in the SEA and the Maastricht Treaty. Many of the objectives outlined in the SEA and the Maastricht Treaty were met during the 1990s and in the initial years of the twenty-first century treaty amendments and member state influence have extended areas of European integration.

This chapter also overviews these amendments and discusses their formulation and impacts in terms of Europeanization and European integration. Chapter 6 identifies the links between European integration procedures and Europeanization in practical terms. It achieves this through an investigation of policy-making institutions and linkages between the domestic and EU levels through interest groups.

Through the pursuit of the SEM, the EU organized a structured system of legal rules with its own sources, and its own institutions and procedures for making, interpreting and enforcing those rules. The treaties have incrementally created an evolutionary legal system, which on the entry into force of each treaty became an integral part of the legal system of the member states. This has implications for domestic institutions relating to financial services and theoretical perspectives. Such is made explicit when direct lobbying of EU institutions constitutes an important part of the policy-making process within the EU and has the effect of increasing supranational autonomy over the interests of member states. There has been a rapid expansion of such activities over the last decade and Chapter 6 identifies supranationality in EU institutions and the extensive use of interest groups in legislation formulation. Interest groups will be defined as non-governmental organizations (NGOs) that attempt to have an influence on public policy. They are entities that provide an institutional linkage between sectors and government.

There is an interaction between the treaties and the policy-making process, for example, the SEA created an impetus for the use of interest groups. With QMV and the SEM programme, lobbying in Brussels became imperative. This again has implications regarding theory and some commentators consider that sovereignty has increasingly been ceded to the European institutions and that decision-making in the EU is a balance between intergovernmental and supranational institutions. Furthermore, following the changes brought about by the SEA and the Maastricht Treaty, Europeanization has become more explicit in terms of uploading and downloading.

Overall, this part provides a historical study of the EU both pre- and post-euro in which the environment for European financial services was, and is, being constructed. The SEM and EMU are the backdrop and in many cases the impetus for the harmonization of financial services. They are intrinsic elements in the ongoing process of European integration and Europeanization.

This part also identifies the interaction between European integration theory and European integration processes and how this interaction assists in an explanation of Europeanization. It explains how the financial services sector participates in the European integration process and plays a part in shaping institutions and legislation, as well as being the recipient of these changes. This part illustrates the interaction between politics and economics in European integration and draws on a number of the above theories to explain the phenomenon in more detail. The following part concentrates on the influence member states have had on the EU, the financial services sector and the impacts the EU has had on member states in terms of insurance, banking and capital and security markets directives and regulations.

Part III

Part three investigates and explains how European integration in financial services is closely linked to European integration processes in general through the SEM and EMU. The previous section provided an outline of the rationale behind the creation of the euro and Eurozone and explained how this was an extension of the SEM. This part explains how the development of financial services legislation at the EU level is as an example of European integration and this will incorporate aspects of neo-functionalism in the context of supranationalism and spillover as well as aspects of multilevel governance. It also identifies how the idea of Europeanization can be seen as an outcome of European integration and how this may be explained through financial services reforms at the domestic level. It also indicates that Europeanization can be conceptualized as uploading to the EU through national or sub-national actors; this is also based on interpretations of neo-functionalism and intergovernmentalism. This provides the basis of an in-depth study of financial services at both the European and domestic levels and identifies the interaction between unity and diversity in the EU and further builds on the Hegelian concept of recognition. The study achieves this through identifying institutional change at both European and domestic levels. Finally, even though this project sees Europeanization as the changes taking place in member states then outlines processes of institutional change that may identify how/why this takes place, different conceptualizations of Europeanization are inclusive rather than exclusive (this is explained in more detail in Chapter 3). Chapter 7 deals with the situation in terms of uploading as Europeanization and European integration in the European financial services sector. Furthermore, negotiations and discussions relating to shared beliefs can be identified through interest group intermediation and EU policy-making institutions.

Chapter 7 identifies instances of uploading, for instance prior to the SEM UK financial service regulatory structures were relatively liberal in relation to other EU member states with supervision based on self-regulation. Other member states had different regulatory structures that ranged from state-controlled sectors like Greece, Portugal and Italy; highly regulated sectors like Germany and France and more liberal sectors such as the Netherlands and Luxembourg (the British regulatory structure was in this category). Overall, there were different regulatory structures throughout the EU in the 1980s. However, through uploading individual perspectives through interest groups a general perception was reached regarding levels of regulation in the EU. In the 1980s member states had different beliefs regarding supervision however, by the end of the 1990s, there was some convergence of these beliefs. Agreed legislation moved the regulatory structures away from self-regulation and state-control and identified a means by which shared beliefs could be realized in the market structure (for further discussion see Howell, 1999, 2000). This chapter identifies this process in relation to uploading during the late 1980s and early 1990s member states. It indicates implications for the financial services sector in relation to participation in the EU policy-making process. It draws together the theoretical propositions and illustrates how the empirical data informs our understanding of European integration theory and practice.

Chapter 8 builds on the formulation of shared beliefs and identifies how this is paradoxical. Indeed, the chapter provides an illustration of the dichotomy between the unitary nature of European integration and the diversity of Europeanization. A directive or regulation constructed at the EU level has to be implemented at the domestic level. This leaves room for interpretation and inclusion of cultural differentiation at the domestic level. The question is, does this cause a difficulty in the construction of a SEM and EMU or can such differentiation be overcome? This chapter identifies the rationale behind regulation especially in an area where the investment and protection of assets are involved. Financial regulation is concerned with three areas; products, intermediaries and markets. Divergence exists among regulators regarding product types, intermediary supervision and the extent of equity and transparency in relation to efficiency and liquidity. Indeed, such divergences would be apparent prior to the European legislation and to an extent still exist following domestic implementation. The interaction between European integration and Europeanization can inform us how far sovereignty and cultural tradition are actually compromised in this context; again the theoretical perspectives will enhance these explanations. Chapter 9 locates further member state uploading regarding the formulation of a SEM in financial services. Furthermore, the chapter overviews the development of the FSAP and the role of financial services authorities in the European integration and Europeanization process. Chapter 10 deals with downloading aspects of Europeanization through case studies of the United Kingdom, Poland, Germany and Italy. This chapter takes one member state from each of the categories outlined in Chapter 7 and one accession state (Poland). It then analyses the levels of downloading in relation to previous uploading and European integration.

Conclusion

In general, Part III identifies the differential between European integration and Europeanization in terms of downloading (En1), uploading (En2), crossloading (En3) and 'content' regarding individual member states in the financial services sector (each of these are discussed in more detail in Part I, Chapter 3). The way each member state has implemented directives and regulations is identified in the context of unity and diversity. Problems exist in this context because one has to determine what has been an outcome of Europeanization and what has been an outcome of other variables, for example, globalization. Uploading on a macro and micro level, European integration processes and downloading of EU policy are used to understand and explain the ongoing evolution of the EU. Indeed, Europeanization is considered as 'situation' and 'process'. The philosophies and the theories will enable greater explanatory power and further understanding of the interaction between European integration and Europeanization and provide greater insight into the role and nature of financial services in the construction/evolution of the EU.

Part I

Philosophical Perspectives and Theoretical Frameworks

Based on philosophical perspectives identified by Kant and Hegel Part I develops a theoretical framework that can be empirically verified in specific domains of European integration. This part argues that the European project is premised on ideas relating to civil constitution and that this may be achieved through notions of recognition. Indeed, grand theories relating to European integration incorporate these ideas. However, grand theories came under criticism in the 1960s and 1970 because they failed to predict and were difficult to verify in a positivist context. This led to the development of meso theories such as Europeanization and a re-assessment of what social science theory was able to achieve. Positivist notions of prediction were challenged and through a post-positivist constructivist mix, meso and substantive theory provided more incisive theoretical explanations of social science in general and European integration in particular. This section outlines this process in relation to Europeanization, European integration theory and European integration process.

In this study the political philosophy, grand, meso and substantive theory are closely interrelated because reality and theory develop through interactions between historical environments, institutions and individuals. In this way the study makes three discrete points, each of which has an impact on the empirical study undertaken in the rest of the book. First, social actors in a changing historical and social context construct reality and theory. Second, social scientists continually develop the concepts they employ, as the limitations of these concepts become explicit. Third, social scientists cannot be objective impassive analysts; they themselves are part of the construction process, as communal values change theory is re-assessed in relation to these changes (George, 1976).

Because of the criticisms levelled at neo-functionalism and intergovernmentalism this chapter re-assesses these grand theories in the context of historical change and social scientists value based re-formulations of European integration theory. It argues that predictive theory in the social sciences is difficult if not impossible to formulate, consequently that grand theory such as neo-functionalism, be seen as a means of 'organising concepts', 'selecting relevant facts' and determining how the 'narrative should be constructed' (ibid.).

1
Recognizing Civil Constitutions: Hegel and Kant as the Basis of Integration Theory?

Introduction

This study bases its understanding of the European Union (EU), European integration and Europeanization on Kantian and Hegelian political philosophy and philosophy of history (for further see Arendt, 1989; Hampsher-Monk, 1995; Hegel, 1967, 1977; Kant 1995a,b; Kojeve, 1980; Ringmar, 1995). The intention of this chapter and part is to provide some insight into international relations theories relating to European integration and illustrate how these, impact on concepts of Europeanization in both practical and theoretical ways. Fundamentally, this chapter argues that elements of European integration and Europeanization developed through the Kantian concept of the international 'civil constitution' and Hegelian interpretations of the state and 'recognition'. As we deal with the euro and EU Enlargement with both existing and prospective members prepared to give up sovereignty to be part of the EU, Kant's civil constitution and Hegel's recognition and master–slave relationship can inform the theoretical debate and comment on the practicalities of European integration.

Kant and Hegel provide the basis of a number of European integration theories, which are covered in Chapter 2. This study considers that European integration theories developed out of functionalism and realism, which were based on the Kantian concept of the international 'civil constitution' (Kant, 1995b, see *Idea for a*

Universal History With a Cosmopolitan Purpose, pp. 41–53 and *Perpetual Peace,* 1995a, pp. 93–115) and Hegelian interpretations of the state and recognition (Hegel, 1967). Hegelian 'recognition' can provide a bridge between realist and functional understandings of integration and the basis of conceptualizations of Europeanization. Indeed, to fully understand European integration and Europeanization it is important to comprehend the direction that on-going debates have taken, and to how in relation to these, the theoretical frameworks have evolved and been applied.

Universal history and perpetual peace

Kant (1995a) argued that no 'conclusion of peace shall be considered valid as such if it was made with a secret reservation of the material for a future war' (p. 93). He considered that to achieve perpetual peace, it was necessary for it to be formally instituted and through a legal 'civil constitution' based on three principles:

> firstly, the principle of *freedom* for all members of society (as men); secondly, the principle of the *dependence* of everyone upon a single common legislation (as subjects); and thirdly, the principle of legal quality for everyone (as citizens) ... a constitution based on cosmopolitan right, in so far as individuals and states, co-existing in an external relationship of mutual influences, may be regarded as citizens of a universal state of mankind (*ius cosmopoliticum*). (ibid., pp. 98–9)

He investigated how human beings could become 'good' citizens through the development of the 'good' constitution. Kant (1995b) first identified these ideas through outlining nine propositions that indicated a guiding purpose for history.

Overall, Kant (1995b) argued that human action is determined by natural laws and history gives an account of these. Individual action is ambiguous and inconsistent but if we generalize human action it may be possible to identify the slow development of humanity's capacities or abilities. Neither individuals nor nations imagine that as they pursued their own ends, they are unwittingly guided by a course intended by nature. They promote an end that, even if they were fully aware, would not interest them. Indeed, because humans do not seem to follow a plan of their own, philosophers look for a plan in nature or history. Kant (1995b) identified this ultimate end for history, in that the natural capacities of a creature are destined to develop completely. In human beings that natural capacity is reason, which cannot be realized by the individual, but may be fully developed by the species. Reason requires trial, practice, instruction and a generational approach to knowledge accumulation. Furthermore, 'nature has willed that man should produce entirely by his own initiative everything which goes beyond the mechanical ordering of his animal existence' (Kant, 1995b, p. 43). Nature has given humanity free will to produce everything it needs in terms of food, clothing, security and defence. 'It seems as if nature intended that man, once he had finally worked his way up ... to inner perfection ... [he/she] should be able to take for himself the entire credit ... and have only himself to thank for it' (ibid., p. 43). Kant considered that nature may be more concerned with humanity's self-esteem than its straightforward well-being (ibid.). In this way, humanity works for the good of future generations; as individuals we are ephemeral, as a species we could be immortal and it is by our improvement through the generations that we may completely develop our natural capacities.

Nature employs antagonisms to bring about legal structures or a governed social order. Kant (1995b) argued that through the *unsocial sociability* of humans social order is created. Humans want to live in a community but at the same time be an individual. Humans want to direct everything in relation to their own ideas. However, as they are likely to resist others in pursuing these ends they also expect resistance to their own endeavours. Resistance and the expectation of the resistance from others, overcomes the human tendency to be lazy, driving the individual to attain social worth and status among peers. As talents are gradually cultivated we see the first step away from barbarism towards culture. 'Nature should thus be thanked for fostering social incompatibility, enviously competitive vanity, and insatiable desires for possessions or even power' (ibid., p. 45). 'The greatest problem for the human species, the solution of which nature compels him to seek, is that of attaining a civil society which can administer justice universally' (ibid., p. 45). Nature identifies an ultimate problem for humanity, the creation and formulation of the just society or a 'perfectly just civil constitution' and only through a solution to this 'will nature accomplish its other intentions with our species' (ibid., p. 46).

Through necessity humans are forced to enter a state of restriction. Individuals bring this imposition on themselves, because it is impossible for them to live for long in a state of wild freedom. However, once enclosed in this situation, the same wild inclinations are beneficial. 'All the culture and art which adorn mankind and the finest social order man creates are fruits of his own unsociability. For it is compelled by its own nature to discipline itself, and thus, by enforced art to develop completely the germs which nature implanted' (ibid.). The just civil constitution is the last and most difficult problem that humanity has to resolve. The problem is that humans have self-will and this needs to be broken. Humans need to be forced to obey so that all can be free. But obey whom? Where will the master be found? Paradoxically, the 'highest authority has to be just in itself' but ultimately human (ibid., p. 46). Consequently, a perfect solution is impossible and nature only requires us to pursue and approximate the ideal. Furthermore, 'why this task must be the last to be accomplished is that man needs for it a correct conception of the nature of a possible constitution, great experience tested in many affairs of the world and above all else a good will prepared to accept the findings of his experience. But three factors such as these will not easily be found in conjunction, and if they are, it will only happen at the last stage and after many unsuccessful attempts' (ibid., p. 47).[1] Many types of constitution will need to be assessed and most will prove unsuccessful. However, through trial and error across many different situations and humanity's belief and confidence in self, the ideal civil constitution will ultimately be realized.

As a species, through its own endeavours, humanity will realize the ultimate problem set by nature. However, as well as a civil constitution between individuals 'the problem of ... law governed relationships with other states' needs to be solved and until this is dealt with the ideal civil constitution cannot be realized. Each state expects the same antagonisms that forced them into a legally governed civil state. What is the point of developing a civil constitution within states if in external relations it and other states are in a position of unrestricted freedom? Once again nature employs humanity's *unsocial sociability* as a means of overcoming this difficulty. Through antagonisms humanity will eventually reach a level of calm and peace. War and the preparation for war initially drive states to make imperfect attempts at creating a civil constitution. However, 'after many devastation's ... [states] take the step which reason could have suggested to them with out so many sad experiences, that of abandoning a lawless state of savagery and entering a federation of peoples' (ibid., p. 47). In this context, security is derived from the federation of a united power made up of united wills. Indeed, following the failures of historical attempts at constitutions on an international level and the devastation in Europe brought about by two world wars, one may see the EU as an attempt to create a civil constitution and federation at the regional level. States are forced into making the same decision individuals made; they are forced to renounce brutish freedom for a civil constitution. However, one may argue that political communities are formed through lucky accident rather than historical course. In response to this, Kant (1995b) examined whether nature was purposive or purposeless.

The purposeless state of savagery stunted the development of human beings natural capacities. Eventually, barbarism forced humans to leave this state and enter a civil constitution and their natural capacities developed further. The same may be said of states because again natural capacities are stunted in exactly the same way. Armament production and preparations for war and the destruction and depredation of those wars hinder states. One only has to look at the human loss and destruction of Europe that was brought about by two world wars to see this. However, these evils have some benefit for they compel humanity to seek out perpetual peace and provide 'a cosmopolitan system of general political security' (p. 49). 'Perpetual peace is *guaranteed* by no less an authority than the great artist *nature* herself (*natura daedala rerum*). The mechanical process of nature visibly exhibits the purposive plan of producing concord among men, even against their will and by means of their discord' (Kant, 1995a, p. 108). In this context nature is purposive. This is made clear by Kant in his Eighth Proposition where he argued that '(t)he history of the human race as a whole can be regarded as the realisation of a hidden plan of nature to bring about an internally – and for this purpose also externally – perfect political constitution as the only state within which all natural capacities of mankind can be developed completely' (Kant, 1995b, p. 50). Furthermore, in the Ninth Proposition Kant argued that humanity may further the purpose of nature. It is assumed that nature is purposeful and that history has a purposeful end and that humans have freedom within this even though this freedom unintentionally works towards nature's end. According to Kant it was useless to assume that free acts of will were undetermined, that an action is free when it is not determined (Ward, 1972). Through the history of enlightened nations we shall discover the means to attain natures' direction. 'We shall discover a regular process of improvement in the political constitutions of our continent' (Kant, 1995a, p. 52). Continually concentrating our attention on the civil constitution and 'the mutual relations among states' (ibid.). History provided us with the means of improving the civil constitution. A constitution is elevated then overthrown, however, the seed of enlightenment always survived and this prepared the way for further improvement. A plan of nature for humanity opens up a comforting prospect in that through the realization of natural capacities in the form of reason and learning from our mistakes human destiny can be fulfilled.

Subjective and objective recognition: identifying self in the EU

For Hegel the good life involved the adoption of social roles and participation in social institutions. Usually the state is understood to encapsulate an ideal institution, which allows self-consciousness to become spirit. However, Hegel does not argue that institutions are rational in themselves, they are not the unfolding of reason themselves but entities that are made rational by humanity. It is humanity that reason which institutions are necessary for a modern society.

Hegel (1977) argued that traditional philosophy was concerned with acceptance or rejection and that the philosophers, of his day, failed to comprehend how the diversity of philosophical systems illustrated 'the progressive unfolding of truth' (ibid., p. 2). Hegel outlined his idea of dialectics through his philosophical system. 'The bud disappears in the bursting forth of the blossom, and one might say that the former is refuted by the latter; similarly, when the fruit appears, the blossom in its turn is shown up as a false manifestation of the plant, and the fruit now emerges as the truth of it instead' (ibid.). This example indicated that each part of the process is on the one hand distinct, but on the other fluid and holistic. Each component of the process is necessary and mutually dependent on the other, which for Hegel was also apparent in the world of ideas. Hegel argued that an individual,

> who rejects a philosophical system ... does not usually comprehend
> what he is doing in this way: and he who grasps the contradiction
> between them ... does not, as a general rule, know how to free it
> from its one-sidedness, or maintain it in its freedom by recognising
> the reciprocally necessary moments that take shape as conflict and
> seeming incompatibility. (ibid.)

Hegel's philosophy can be used to analyse and understand international relations. Indeed, through Hegelian dialectics we can move from a realist interpretation of international relations to one that accepts international law and the international community. Furthermore, if humanity is the rational agent and institutions the outcome of this rationality then different institutions were appropriate for different situations. This interpretation removes the emphasis from the state as an ideal structure and provides arguments for changes in institutional and social structures.

Phenomenology described the development of 'natural phenomenal consciousness ... by way of science and philosophy toward the absolute knowledge of the absolute' (Hegel, 1977, p. 2). Hegel considered that truth may be discovered through philosophy and history; philosophy because it indicated what should be in the world and history because it identified the content of the world as it unfolded over time. Indeed, 'it is in spirit and the process of its development, that is the substance of history' (Hegel, 1988, p. 19).

The starting point is the naïve mind's emergent comprehension of external reality. Mind becomes aware of itself through subjective and objective self-consciousness. Subjective awareness of self is not enough to enable self-consciousness because this is unable to sufficiently inform human beings about what they are like in the world. Humans need a complimentary objective stance. Self needs an objective recognition of its own consciousness to provide an understanding of its own reality. Only another human being can provide this; through reflecting for that consciousness a sense of its own external being.

In this context, objective truth lies in mutuality of recognition. 'Others' define 'self' and 'self' defines 'self' in relation to the definition of 'others'. Community defines 'self' and 'self' defines community. 'The savage lives in himself; sociable man, always outside himself, is capable of living only in the opinion of other; and so to speak, derives the sentiments of his own existence solely from their judgement' (Rousseau, cited in Pippin, 1997, p. 93). The objective 'self' accepts Rousseau's identification of the situation and provides a potential means of dealing with it (ibid.). Hegel argued that the transition is not that straightforward because initially the existence of the 'other' will be perceived as a threat to being and a negation of 'self' this may be identified as a form of Kant's *unsocial sociability*. Recognition in the EU based on *mutual recognition* of rules, regulations and cultural differences allows synthesis of member state differentiation and provided an important legal mechanism that assists the process of European integration.[2]

Before the subject is confronted by 'other' he/she existed in a world of things. Consequently, the subject deals with the 'other' by treating it as a thing and validates its own image as an entity in control of a sea of things. Because the subject does not yet see itself in an objective form, it treats other consciousness as entities to be controlled. This is illustrated in the Hobbesian 'state of nature' and imperfect Kantian 'civil constitution'. Furthermore, the rationale behind war may be perceived in this situation, with 'self' and 'other', incorporating different tribes or nations.

Subduing 'other' leads to conflict and enslavement and undermines opportunities to enable full self-consciousness. The form of 'recognition' initially understood is subordination or reduction of the 'other' and through a life–death struggle in the pursuit of recognition social life and political union emerge. Death of 'other' does not solve the problem of 'recognition'. Victory must be attained and 'recognition' accepted before the death of 'other'. Indeed, a master–slave relationship arises, which underpins the emergence of 'recognition', self-consciousness and social life. Hegel does not mean that all relationships are enslaving but that this was the dialectical basis for political, economic, social relationships and so on. The struggle for 'recognition' was an ongoing process and a continuing feature of social life. For Hegel the master–slave relationship was not simply an early social structure. 'The development of social relationships … is not … simply … one leading from one to another, but self inclusive, each earlier stage incorporating a higher form than the earlier ones, the master–slave relationship is a protean source of the various relationships, political, economic, social and sexual' (Hampsher-Monk, 1995, p. 426).

Initially, through victory the master seems to have ensured 'recognition'. However, to ensure self-awareness consciousness needs the recognition of an equal. The master has only won by reducing the 'other' to the status of a thing in the world. Because the master existed in a world of things there had been no progression of consciousness. 'His consciousness has progressed no further than its existence in a world of unconscious objects' (ibid., p. 427). Recognition is needed from someone of equal status.

On the other hand, the slave is conscious of another independent mind in the world. Although forced to recognize the master or 'other' the slave progresses from a subjective conceptualization of 'self' towards an objective awareness of 'self'. Through synthesizing a consciousness experienced subjectively in 'self', and a consciousness experienced objectively, in another, the slave is able to have an objective awareness of the 'self's' subjectivity. The positive aspect of enslavement relates to an understanding of the futility of ego, which clears the consciousness and identifies the importance of labour.

Reality for the master is defined by consumption whereas through work 'the slave ... increases his awareness of himself and his relationship to an initially intractable Nature in the course of transforming it for his master' (Hampsher-Monk, 1995, p. 427). As noted above, this transition is not easy, as the individual primarily perceives others as a threat to 'self' (ibid.). However, Hegel continually indicated that humans are unable to organize a total concept of 'self' unless this is in relation to 'others'.

Differences between master and slave are gradually overcome by the slave's ability to progress. Through labour the slave becomes educated and develops a fully formed 'self' in terms of personal capacities and comprehension of the world. 'In this way recognition and personal identity came to be seen as achievements ... Hegel envisioned social relations as becoming increasingly equal as more and more individuals freed themselves from both the determination of nature and the ... subjugation ... imposed by others' (Ringmar, 1995, p. 94). Hegel identified freedom of will as the greatest good, a freedom where the will has itself as its object. Indeed, if anyone speaks of free will without referring to the will that is absolutely free he or she is only referring to the potential or capacity for freedom and not of the free will (Hegel, 1967). Only in a truly objective freedom 'is the will by itself without qualification, because then it is related to nothing except itself and so is released from dependence on everything else' (ibid., p. 30). Free will is consequently universalized because 'the difference between its implicit character and its subjective awareness of itself, or between its universality and its exclusive individuality' have been resolved (ibid., p. 31). Such a situation may be identified in the relationship the reflective agent has with rational institutions of right. In this context, property, contract and morality are implicit with a natural will and such implicitly aim at becoming a full free will and so realizes itself in the institutions that make possible and realize freedom. Ultimately, the rational agent commits self to the logic of abstract right in terms of property and contract, which provides moral regard for the 'other'. Moral beings tie their identity to others through binding themselves to certain institutions by some form of constitution. This again allows generalization. 'The moral life is first and foremost a corporate life lived in a community, and there is a sense in which no community can afford to allow its individual members absolute liberty of choice on whether to accept prevailing moral rules' (Walsh, 1969, p. 77). Regulations are constructed by humanity and subsequently they should be able to be altered by humanity. However, they are not made by individuals nor should they be changed by individuals but by groups and humans in general.

'Recognition' may also be related to nation-states in their quest for acknowledgement on the international stage. In the ethical community the individual has a right to recognition and the law guarantees that a people are given the opportunity to develop. Indeed, the law is an institution and structure that provides meaning for our lives 'we submit ourselves to a certain way of life, and as a result we come to see ourselves as persons of a certain kind ... By following the rules ... a person is making demands on the people around her to recognise her as a legitimate member of their group' (Ringmar, 1995, p. 95).

The debate at the international level revolves around realist and functionalist arguments. Realism is based on Hobbesian and a specific Hegelian interpretation of the state and international relations. Hegel (1967) argued that '(i)nternational law springs from the relations between autonomous state ... The nation-state is mind in its substantive rationality and immediate actuality and is therefore the absolute power on earth' (p. 212). In this context, Hegel seems to deny international law and provided the basis for a realist interpretation of international relations, which considered that nation-states were sovereign entities that brought about change in international relations. However, Hegel also outlined a defence of international law in that law was more than a construct for telling right from wrong. It was also a means of 'determining the class of subjects to whom the law itself applies' and defined the 'constitution of individual identities' (Ringmar, 1995, p. 92).

Ringmar (1995) undertook a historical analysis, which identified a number of problems with the realist interpretation of Hegel and considered that in a period of state creation legal requirements are crucial. Features of law contributed to this because laws give substantive context to actions that political entities perform; and provided standards by which political institutions may be recognized as entities of a certain type. Indeed, the EU provided a legal structure that potential members adhere to, so they are recognized as democratic entities by the existing membership. In this way, member states are recognized as things of a certain kind and member states have both subjective and objective perspectives of 'self'.

Conclusion

In *Universal History*, Kant argued that, 'all natural capacities of a creature are destined to evolve completely to their natural end [and] the unsociable sociability of man' moving towards the 'achievement of universal civil society which administers laws among men' is the highest problem nature assigns to humanity (ibid., p. 43). Only once a civil society has been attained can nature's other problems be solved. Humans need to exist within society because this creates a feeling of being more than human (as more than the developed form of their natural capacities). At the same time humans are unsociable because they feel hostility to those around them and expect hostility in return. It is this process that forces humans to protect themselves by aspiring to hold rank among their peers. Necessity, forces humanity into curbing its natural aspirations to ensure a peaceful existence, unsociability initiates the 'just civil constitution' and this incorporates laws to which all are answerable and no one is above. However, Kant recognized that one nation may attain a 'just civil constitution' but unfortunately antagonisms would still exist between states (ibid.). 'The problem of establishing a perfect civil constitution is dependent on the problem of a lawful external relation among states and cannot be solved without a solution to the latter problem' (ibid., p. 48). Each state will expect the same antagonisms, which forced it into seeking its own civil constitution. Through war and the threat of war, the full potential of humanity cannot be realized: consequently humanity is forced to seek the means of ensuring equilibrium. Through self-interest humanity is forced to accept mutual existence. This text considers that this is the basis of process in terms of European integration: mutuality and peace created through self-interest. Through self-interest humanity accepts and fosters social and political union.

This chapter has argued that Kantian and Hegelian thought underpin past, present and in some instances future attempts at equilibrium, peaceful coexistence and co-operation. The concept of the League of Nations and a united Europe were initiated through the pursuit of a civil constitution to ensure perpetual peace. The premise of the European Coal and Steel Community (ECSC) was peace: its objective was to alleviate the prospect of war in Europe by controlling the products necessary to conduct a war. Through the pursuit of perpetual peace, Kant perceives a world civil constitution; this work contends that the EU fits into such an understanding and that through Hegelian recognition it may be seen as an evolutionary or dialectical movement away from the nation-state towards another form of political institution or community.

By transferring identity formation towards the state Hegel can shed new light on international law, the EU and its membership. Through identity formation, the EU is constructing another political community one that is not international but beyond the nation-state. Indeed, recognition is forming a supranational political community.

In the aftermath of two world wars the EU was not about subjugation and enforced coalescence, but freedom of choice and integration. Democratic states voluntarily transferred sovereignty to supranational institutions. To achieve this states became aware of subjective and objective recognition in their interpretations of 'self'. European imperialism, subjugation of other cultures and conflict failed to provide Europe with a full understanding of 'self'. Through this interpretation of Hegel we may find the dialectical step from the nation-state to the Kantian 'civil constitution'. Through recognition we may identify the bridge between conflict and peaceful co-operation.

Kantian political thought incorporated a peaceful process directed at a peaceful end that wished to ensure a 'civil constitution' under the auspices of perpetual peace (Kant, 1995a,b). Furthermore, there is a growing propensity towards Hegelian 'recognition' as member states adhere to principles of human rights and democracy in their quest to become members of the EU (Ringmar, 1994). Fundamentally, it is possible to argue that through the Hegelian concept of 'recognition' we are moving towards a Kantian 'civil constitution'. '(I)ndividuals can attain their ends only in so far as they themselves determine their knowing, willing and acting in a universal way and make themselves links in this chain of social connexions. In these circumstances, the interest of the Idea – an interest of which these members of civil society are as such unconscious – lies in the process whereby their singularity and their natural condition are raised, as a result of the necessities imposed by nature as well as of arbitrary needs, to formal freedom and formal universality of knowing and willing the – process whereby their particularity is educated up to subjectivity' (Hegel, 1967, p. 124). Hegelian recognition could be perceived as a means of a transposition between realist and functional understandings of integration, between the realist interpretation of Hegel and the Kantian civil constitution. Hegelian recognition is a mechanism that could bring about perpetual peace and the just civil constitution. The following chapter investigates theoretical issues relating to the EU and draws on some of the political philosophy discussed in this chapter to bridge the divide between theory and practice.

2
Re-assessing European Integration Theory

Introduction

Chapter 1 identified abstract notions of human and international relations and argued that European integration theory and practice could be based on philosophical perspectives identified by Kant and Hegel. That there was a Hobbesian perspective of Hegelian thought in terms of realism, which dialectically moves towards a Kantian perspective, Hegelian 'recognition' and an objective as well as subjective consciousness in the formation of a 'civil constitution'. Civil constitution and recognition provide a philosophical framework, which can be used to explain motives and rationales for European integration. Cause and effect or dependent and independent variables may be posited but are impossible to verify, prediction is asserted in some parts of the philosophies, for example, the guiding hand of history, but are difficult to test from a positivist perspective. Indeed, it may be argued that the best these frameworks can achieve is to provide general explanations that point in the direction of grand theories of European integration and international relations. This chapter deals with these theories in more detail and identifies the extent to which functionalist and realist perspectives may be considered as explanatory frameworks or predictive tools.

Over the last 50 years the drivers of European integration and rationales for the process have been discussed and debated in terms of perpetual peace and economic regeneration. Indeed, the concept of perpetual peace underpins the notion of the Kantian civil constitution and economic regeneration formed the basis of recognition.

Initially, the discussions revolved around functionalism (Claude, 1965; Mitrany, 1943, 1944, 1965, 1970, 1975a,b,c; Sewell, 1966) and neo-functionalism, which seemed to provide a succinct explanation of European integration (Haas, 1958, 1964, 1971, 1975, 1976; Lindberg, 1963, 1967). However, during the 1960s understandings of European integration based on functionalism and neo-functionalism were challenged. It is generally considered that the actions of Charles de Gaulle during the 1960s, led to the reassertion of realism through an emphasis on intergovernmentalism as neo-functionalism was challenged for its deterministic nature and absence of a dependent variable.[1] However, George (1976) argued that the main impetus behind the challenge to neo-functionalism was related to a criticism of grand theories in general and recognition that a positivist approach to social science was flawed. This chapter identifies differences and similarities between grand theories that have an international dimension and grand European integration theories. Realism and functionalism attempted to explain at the international level – intergovernmentalism and neo-functionalism at the European. Indeed, through a change in emphasis that is, from the international to European we witness an attempt to provide specificity and positivist explanation. However, with changes in the empirical nature of the EU and because of their abstract dimensions both neo-functionalism and intergovernmentalism were unable to provide positivist explanation in terms of prediction and cause and effect and were consequently criticized as European integration theories. Furthermore, the chapter also introduces meso level theories such as Europeanization, multilevel and state-centric governance, which especially in the context of Europeanization and substantive theory, are discussed in more detail in Chapter 3.

Grand theories of international relations and European integration

The realist critique emphasized the importance of the nation-state in the process of international politics and is based on a Hobbesian model of anarchy and power. Indeed, this interpretation provided the basis for one of Hegel's interpretations of international relations.

For realism, theory consists in ascertaining facts and giving them meaning through reason. It assumes that the character of a foreign policy can be ascertained only through the examination of political acts performed and of the foreseeable consequences of these acts. Thus we can find out what statesmen have actually done, and from the foreseeable consequences of their acts we can surmise what their objectives might have been. (Morgenthau, 1973, p. 4)

Indeed, the methodological approach used by realists is positivist and one that could, fail to identify important variables when explaining integration.

Based on the realist critique, intergovernmentalism considered a number of points regarding European integration. First, regional integration should take global criteria into account. Second, the real drivers in the process of European integration were member states and these would remain committed to national interest. Third, transference between low and high politics would never occur and integration would be condoned in technical fields to ensure mutual benefit but never move into areas like defence, monetary policy and national security (George, 1994). Intergovermentalists (or neo-realists) considered that member states were self-interested and sovereign and incapable of acting in a collective manner.

Schmitter (1996) argued that although nation-states regarded each other with hostility they could work together 'through the formation of regimes, but only to enhance or protect their respective power in the interstate system. Any action which either diminished that capability, deliberately or assigned it irrevocably to another polity is (theoretically) incomprehensible' (p. 3). In general, the main emphasis of intergovernmentalism was that interstate bargaining and national preferences in terms of high politics provided the main impetus and rationales for European integration (Moravcsik, 1991, 1993, 1998).

Moravcsik (1991, 1993, 1998) provided evidence that the primary source of integration resided with member states and in this context takes an intergovernmental stance. 'Liberal-intergovernmentalism divides the EU decision process into two stages each of which is grounded in one of the classical integration theories' (Hix, 1999, p. 15). Initially domestic actors demand European integration and as with neo-functionalism these 'actors have economic interests and compete for these interests to be promoted by national governments in EU decision-making' (ibid.). Integration is driven by inter-state bargaining, states are unitary actors and supranational institutions have limited impact on outcomes (ibid.). 'European integration resulted from a series of rational choices made by national leaders who consistently pursued economic interests – primarily the interests of powerful economic producers and secondarily the macro economic preferences of ruling governmental coalitions – that evolve slowly in response to structural incentives in the global economy' (Moravcsik, 1998, p. 3). However, Richardson (1996) argued that to fully understand European integration it was necessary to take low politics as seriously as high politics. European integration was 'not simply the outcome of inter-state bargaining' (p. 5), but a complex process involving numerous actors and procedures, which can involve federal, functional and neo-functional variables as well as realist or intergovernmental processes.

The modern understanding of functionalism in the realms of international relations has been commonly attributed to David Mitrany. Functionalism denied a Hobbesian state of conflict and outlined a means by which peaceful international collaboration may be achieved. This strategy is realized through organizations with specific tasks, which evolve as functional needs change. The system incorporated the premise of peaceful co-operation. In a limited sense a functional outcome may produce a pluralist international community where national control is marginalized through functional linkages, or in a wider or more intensive sense, a situation where the nation-state disappears and is replaced by international functional rationality. This is where organizational patterns are undertaken at the most rational level that is, international, continental or regional. Effectively, functionalism is the internationalization of politics, with decision-making carried out at the most rational or functional level. Functionalism does not pursue some form of end result in the context of a political community. Mitrany considered that human beings have no concept of what the end result of integration should encompass, so why invent one? As noted by Popper (1994), the future is open and possibility infinite, humanity is responsible for its future and this given it is our duty to have faith in ourselves and remain optimistic.

Kant may be perceived as functionalist in terms of his pursuit of an international 'civil constitution'. However, he may be considered federalist or neo-functionalist in terms of his wish for an actualization of this. The difference between functionalism and federalism is that the former identifies a process and the latter an end in some form of federal state. Federalism provides for the enlargement of representative government; it allows administration to extend from one to many states (Bosco, 1991; Hodges, 1972).

Unlike functionalism, neo-functionalism argued that integration is more easily realized in a regional setting. Functionalists conceded that a supranational state would keep peace at the regional level. However, it would also create a power bloc and not ensure peace at the international level. In this context, Mitrany criticized European integration. Haas (1971) accepted Mitrany's criticism when he argued that regional integration may lead to a future world made up of fewer and fewer units, each unit with all the power and self-assertion that we associate with classical nationalism. This of course may negate the Kantian objective of perpetual peace and an international civil constitution; but also further it through the realization of the Hegelian perspective with larger units experiencing objective as well as subjective recognition.

Haas (1958, 1964, 1968, 1971) proposed a concept of incremental integration, which was based on his study of the European Coal and Steel Community (ECSC), this placed an emphasis on functional integration. Haas (1958) provided an explanation of the process and progression of European integration through his analysis of supranationality, sub-national interests and spillover. He argued that sub-national actors 'in several distinct national settings are persuaded to shift their loyalties, expectations and political activities toward a new centre, whose institutions possess or demand jurisdiction over the pre-existing national states' (p. 16). This was similar to Lindberg (1963) who considered that European integration was '(a) The process whereby nations forgo the desire and ability to conduct foreign and key domestic policies independently of each other, seeking instead to make joint decisions or to delegate the decision-making process to new central organs; and (b) the process whereby political actors in several distinct settings are persuaded to shift their expectations and political activities to a new centre' (p. 6). In both of these theorists we can identify the shift towards a new political centre or supranational institution and the shift of loyalties by sub-national actors towards this institution. Fundamentally, sub-national interests shift their allegiance to a supranational body and in doing so further develop supranational institutions and provide a stimulus for spillover.

Spillover can be broken down into three types. First, *functional spillover*, which was indicated when integration in one industry/sector created its own impetus and necessitated further integration both in the same, and in other industries/sectors. Second, *cultivated spillover*, which assumed that the European Commission would be pro-active in the management of European integration. Third, *institutional/ political spillover* which 'describes the accretion of new powers and tasks to a central institutional structure' (Haas, cited in Kirchner, 1976, p. 3). There is an interaction between spillover and supranationality in that the 'establishment of supranational institutions designed to deal with functionally specific tasks will set in motion economic, social and political processes which generate pressures towards further integration' (Tranholme-Mikkelson, 1991, p. 4).

Haas (1958) labelled functional spillover the 'expansive logic of sector integration' (p. 243). However, the extent to which changing incentives created by spillover allowed an explanation for task expansion has been a point of contention for neo-functionalists. Nye (1971) argued that the functional linkage of tasks has been a less powerful mechanism than was originally believed to be the case and Lindberg and Scheingold (1971) denied that spillover led to the formation or continuation of the common market.

A further understanding of neo-functionalism was outlined by Schmitter (1971), who argued that European integration was 'the process of transferring exclusive expectations of benefits from the nation-state to some larger entity. It encompasses the process by virtue of which national actors of all sorts (government officials, interest group spokesmen, politicians as well as ordinary people) cease to identify themselves and their future welfare entirely with their own national government and its policies' (p. 238). Webb (1983) argued that European integration had produced a policy-making system that was partially integrated, but that political integration was unlikely and neo-functionalism was obsolete.

Mutimer (1989) revisited neo-functionalism and emphasized the importance of the Single European Act (SEA). However, he eventually dismissed neo-functionalism because 'even in amended form it is not sufficient' (ibid., p. 101). Pedersen (1992) considered that intergovernmentalism should be combined with elements of neo-functionalism to enable a new framework of analysis. Keohane and Hoffman (1990, 1991) emphasized pooling sovereignty rather than transferring it from the member states to supranational institutions. Furthermore, Corbey (1995) amended neo-functionalism and argued that dialectical functionalism provided the impetus for European integration.

Indeed, European integration was 'a process of action (decision to act) and reaction (response to integration). Progress is generated by the mutual interaction of the institutions of the EU, member states, and interest groups, Since integration proceeds in stages, the dialectics of the process has to be given more attention' (pp. 262–3). This has implications for Europeanization especially in terms of uploading which will be discussed in more detail in the following chapter.

Sandholtz (1994) and Sandholtz and Zysman (1989) argued that three groups reshaped the EU: industrial elites, EU institutions and member state governments. Furthermore, Sandholtz (1994) investigated why member states were prepared to give up their currencies and the sovereignty this entails. He argued that membership of the EU defined preference parameters and decisions and that intergovernmentalism alone failed to explain the impact that membership of the EU has on member state preferences, interests and demands. Indeed, if European integration was to be fully understood a combination of approaches was necessary. Along with a call for more empirical studies this was a theme that has also been argued by Tranholme-Mikkelson (1991), George (1994b, 1995), Garrett and Tsebelis (1996), Gehring (1996), Richardson (1996a) and Ugur (1997).

Following an empirical study of European integration over the late 1960s and early 1970s, Kirchner (1976) argued that the 'logic and forces outlined by Haas were generally found to be operative' (p. 4). However, in a later work he contended that neither neo-functionalism nor intergovernmentalism adequately captured 'the existing overlap in decision-making between national and Community authorities, the sharing of joint tasks and interests, and the fusion of competencies between the national and Community level' (Kirchner, 1992, p. 35). Fundamentally, a mix of theories was necessary to explain and understand European integration at a lower level of abstraction than the grand theories would allow.

Meso European integration theory

Petersen (1995) argued that 'the gap remains wide between theoretical models which seek to explain broad patterns of European integration and those which seek to explain the EU's policy-making process' (p. 69). Indeed, because of this gap certain aspects of grand theories were taken up by meso theories and the debate turned towards governance through the arguments initiated by Keohane and Hoffman (1991), Marks (1993) and Marks *et al.* (1996, 1996a). Questions were formed regarding the political order that was emerging in the EU and policy-making investigated through meso theories. Hooghe and Marks (1997), linked neo-functionalism (through supranational actors and interest groups) to multilevel governance and intergovernmentalism to state-centric governance. They concluded that the state-centric approach was not capable of fully explaining European policy-making processes because EU policy-making was multilevel in nature. Indeed, Marks *et al.* (1996) provided an interesting interpretation of their situation and one that may illustrate certain procedures today.

> Multilevel governance does not confront the sovereignty of states directly. Instead of being explicitly challenged states in the European Union are being melded gently into multi-level polity by their leaders and the actions of numerous sub-national and supranational actors. State-centric theorists are right when they argue that states are extremely powerful institutions that are capable of crushing direct threats to their existence. (p. 371)

However, it is not necessary 'to argue that states are on the verge of political extinction to believe that their control of those living in their territories has significantly weakened' (ibid.). It has been suggested that multilevel governance is not a theory but merely an identification that policy is made at different levels. That it is simply a description of policy-making procedures at different levels. Through the utilization of variables from grand theories Europeanization built on explanations forwarded by multilevel governance and provided an extension of the meso theory by mapping the interactions between different levels in both EU and domestic policy-making processes. Indeed based on explanations posited by multilevel governance Europeanization provided a more succinct and clearer explanation of European integration processes.

Conclusion

This chapter has overviewed a number of integration theories relating to European integration, for example, neo-functionalism and intergovernmentalism. The chapter considered that these developed out of functionalism and realism, which were based on the Kantian concept of the international civil constitution and Hegelian interpretations of the state and recognition (Hegel, 1967).

Overall, there is now some agreement that, 'a range of ideas... explain the realities, dynamics and complexities of European integration' (Greenwood, 1997, p. 242). Indeed, the amalgamation of ideas came about following the SEA, Qualified Majority Voting (QMV) and member state uncertainty about where the reassertion of the SEM would lead them. The loss of the veto (in many areas) and uncertainty in the face of supranationality questioned the realist tradition 'of member states as rational utility-maximisers in interstate bargaining, jealousy guarding their sovereignty and calculating the limits to which sovereignty needed to be pooled for their own advantage' (ibid., pp. 242–3). With the renewed emphasis on integration many realized that the EU was undergoing metamorphosis and that this would have 'major implications for the actors, the processes and the outcomes of policy-making at all levels in Europe: supranational, national and sub-national' (Marks *et al.*, 1996, p. 14). This chapter implied that there can be an amalgamation of international relations and European integration theories in furthering our explanations and understandings of European integration process and through multilevel governance and Europeanization this can be extended again. Chapter 3 concentrates on a conceptualization of Europeanization and its relationships with European integration theory and European integration processes.

3
Uploading, Downloading or Crossloading? Conceptualizing Europeanization and European Integration

Introduction

This chapter builds on the previous two chapters in developing an understanding of European integration theory and how this may be applied to European integration processes. Chapter 3 develops a conceptualization of Europeanization in terms of meso and substantive theoretical perspectives – and provides an explanation of the ongoing dialectical relationship between European integration processes, European integration theory and Europeanization. To achieve this, the chapter undertakes two interrelated objectives. First, it re-assesses neo-functionalism and intergovernmentalism as grand European integration theories from a non-positivist perspective and through this re-assessment, bring together elements of positivism and constructivism[1] in a conceptualization of Europeanization. Second, it examines differences and similarities between European integration theory and Europeanization and through a break down of neo-functionalism identifies Europeanization as a meso theory or middle range theory and elements of this as substantive theory (theory developed in relation to the data). This will allow empirical reliability of elements of neo-functionalism through a working conceptualization of Europeanization. 'Recent research on European integration has moved away from "grand scale" theories about the causes and direction of this phenomenon to more middle range theories about the precise terms of change and the impact of EU involvement in the policy-making process of national political systems' (Ashead, 2002, p. 25).

As noted by Ashead (2002), Andersen and Eliassen (2001), Bulmer and Burch (2001), Dyson (1999), George (1976) and Goetz and Hix (2000) as grand theories of European integration came under scrutiny and their problems became explicit, social scientists developed meso theories to deal with their limitations. Europeanization can be perceived as a meso theory particularly in relation to neo-functionalism and intergovernmentalism. Specific meso theories have included historical institutionalism and state-centric and multilevel governance however, there have been criticisms of multilevel governance as a theory in that it only provides descriptions of what is happening in the EU. Through a synthesis of multilevel governance and elements of the grand theories Europeanization attempts to deal with this perceived deficiency.

Olsen (2002) argued that Europeanization was a fashionable term for which there were many definitions. In fact he inquired, that given the uncertainty that surrounded the concept was it worth bothering with? A number of commentators including Olsen considered that it was worth bothering with, even though it needed further exploration, explanation and conceptualization. For further work on this issue, see Bomberg and Peterson (2000), Börzel (1999, 2002, 2003), Börzel and Risse (2000), Buller and Gamble (2002), Bulmer and Burch (2001), Dyson (2000, 2002), Dyson and Goetz (2002), Featherstone and Kazamias (2001), George (2001), Goetz and Hix (2000), Howell (2002, 2003), Ladrech (1994), Olsen (2002), Radaelli (2000) and Risse *et al.* (2001). Dyson and Goetz (2002) pointed out the difficulties relating to Europeanization when they indicated how the term was used in a number of different ways, 'it is sometimes used narrowly to refer to implementation of EU legislation or more broadly to capture policy transfer and learning within the EU. It is sometimes used to identify the shift of national policy paradigms and instruments to the EU level. [Other] ... times it is used in a narrower way to refer to its effects at the domestic level ... or in a more expansive way to include affects on discourse and identities as well as structures and policies at the domestic level' (p. 2).

Initially, this chapter summarizes conceptualizations of Europeanization that have been forwarded over the last decade. Second, it discusses some issues relating to these conceptualizations and provides some independent analysis. Third, it overviews the difficulties relating to the conceptualization of Europeanization in relation to European integration. Overall, this chapter illustrates how by re-assessing neo-functionalism in a multilevel governance context and through differing epistemologies and ontologies, we may enhance our utilization of Europeanization and consequent analysis of the EU processes and European integration theory.

Overviewing Europeanization

Ladrech (1994) provided a starting point when he argued that Europeanization was 'an incremental process reorienting the direction and shape of politics to the degree that EC political and economic dynamics become part of the organisational logic of national logic of national politics and policy-making' (p. 70). This seems to necessitate a process of downloading or top-down procedures, which following some discussion was ultimately forwarded by Börzel and Risse (2000), Buller and Gamble (2002), Hix and Goetz (2000) and George (2001). George (2001) acknowledged that his interpretation of 'Europeanization ... is only part of a larger ... two way process' (p. 1). However, it focused on the impact of the EU on the UK system. Buller and Gamble (2002) also explored wider conceptualizations of Europeanization but ultimately considered it to be 'a situation where distinct modes of European governance have transformed aspects of domestic politics' (p. 17). Fundamentally, they wished to explore whether Europeanization existed at member state level but recognized that outcomes are not inevitable and rely on interactions between member states and the domestic and EU levels (ibid.). In the main, emphasis for these conceptualizations of Europeanization was a concentration on the downloading or top-down perspective or EU effects on domestic policies and legislation. In a similar way, Hix and Goetz (2000) identified European integration as an independent variable and change in domestic systems or Europeanization as dependent variables. This is a useful distinction if Europeanization is the outcome of change at the domestic level however, if the domestic level initiates change in the EU and affects European integration then the variables are reversed. The relationship between European integration and Europeanization is interactive and distinction between the dependent and independent variables obscured. In this way, Europeanization becomes an interactive process, which involves bottom-up and top-down procedures or 'projection' and 'reception'. 'To dissect Europeanisation as reception and projection highlights our view of the relationship between the EU and member-government institutions as iterative and interactive. It is difficult to try to conceive of the relationship in conventional, positivist social science terms i.e. with independent and dependent variables and simple causality if analysis is to capture incrementalism and continuity' (Bulmer and Burch, 2001, p. 78).

Dyson (2002) explained that, 'Europeanization remains a relatively new theoretical interest and has produced more questions than answers' (p. 3). In the same fashion Featherstone and Kazamias (2001) proposed that Europeanization was a 'dynamic process unfolding over time' and through complex interactive variables it provided contradictory, divergent and contingent effects. However, they ultimately argued that Europeanization included both domestic and EU levels of policy-making and stressed the interdependence between the two. Indeed, they 'focus' on the expansion of EU institutions and their policy-making capabilities as well as changes in member states based on such expansions (ibid.). In other words, concentration on downloading alone was not sufficient and uploading and crossloading needed to be considered in an understanding of the EU as 'process'.

A further interpretation of Europeanization can be found in the context of policy transfer. Bomberg and Peterson (2000), for example, examined the links between policy transfer and Europeanization and raised questions regarding Europeanization by stealth. They considered that both areas have become common concepts in the EU policy-making literature although links between them have remained unexplored. They accepted that the EU has a political process embedded in procedures and treaties but investigated the extent that the established process at the EU level still provided the main impetus behind policy-making in Europe.

Finally, there are interpretations of Europeanization that adopt more general concepts which consider it to include 'processes of (a) construction (b) diffusion (c) institutionalization of formal and informal rules, procedures, policy paradigms, styles, "ways of doing things" and shared beliefs and norms which are first defined and consolidated in the making of EU decisions and then incorporated in the logic of domestic discourse, identities, political structures and public policies' (Radaelli, 2000, p. 4). However, these broad definitions lead to an inclusive conceptualization of Europeanization and broker criticisms of 'conceptual stretching'. In this context, Radaelli (2000) argued that Europeanization was difficult to define because, if all things have been touched by Europe, to some extent or other, all things have been Europeanized. If Europeanization can be used to explain 'cultural change, new identity formation, policy change, administrative innovation and even modernisation' (ibid.). It eventually becomes all things to all people and to some extent almost meaningless. For Radaelli (2000) the most appropriate course of action would be to unpack the concept and distinguish between related concepts like convergence, harmonization and political integration. This chapter now unpacks Europeanization in relation to separate definitions and interpretations of the concept in an attempt to render it more useful in comprehending the evolving EU.

Developing and analysing Europeanization

Europeanization has numerous definitions, which some commentators argue detract from its explanatory power and leaves us with a case of 'conceptual stretching' (Radaelli, 2000). To deal with 'conceptual stretching' and levels of inclusion and exclusion this section of the chapter breaks down the theory into constituent parts and proposes three substantive theories of Europeanization with specific 'content' in relation to European integration. Each substantive theory distinguishes between the extent Europeanization can be empirically validated and said to have been a variable in the process of EU and member state transformation. Finally the section identifies the differences and similarities between Europeanization and European integration.

This study conceptualizes Europeanization in the following way: Europeanization 1 (En1) entails downloading or top-down Europeanization and is based on conceptualizations forwarded by Buller and Gamble (2002), Dyson and Goetz (2002), George (2001) and Ladrech (1994). These commentators provide analysis of wider perspectives of Europeanization but emphasize En1 because of its clarity in terms of explanatory power and determination of cause and effect. Europeanization 2 (En2) incorporates uploading or bottom-up Europeanization and is based on conceptualizations indicated by Börzel (2002), Bulmer and Burch (2001), Dyson (1999) and Risse *et al.* (2001). In most instances, these conceptualizations emphasize the creation of the EU policy-making structures, which identify definitions of European integration, rather than the mechanism of domestic uploading. This study also attempts to deal with the distinction between policy transfer and Europeanization through the development of crossloading (En3).

There was some dispute whether Risse *et al.* (2001) identified European integration when they perceived Europeanization as the 'emergence and development at the European level of distinct structures of governance, that is, of political legal and social institutions associated with political problem solving that formalises interactions among the actors, and of policy networks specialising in the creation of authoritative European rules' (p. 3). The emphasis on 'emergence and development' of EU institutions identifies Europeanization in terms of uploading and downloading in terms of 'authoritative European rules'. Indeed, the emphasis on the creation of rules at the EU level moves away from a utilization of Europeanization as purely downloading to one that entails 'the evolution of European institutions that impact on political processes and structures of the member states' (Börzel, 2002, p. 193), where Europeanization incorporates an interactive process in that it involves bottom-up and top-down procedures. However, Risse *et al.* (2001) do not make the distinction between European integration and uploading or downloading explicit, which causes problems when it comes to identifying the differences between Europeanization and European integration.

Differences exist between Europeanization and European integration, however they do continuously interact; for instance the development of the supranational level in the context of evolving institutions can be seen as European integration. Uploading or En2 indicates governments (macro uploading) or sub-national interests (micro uploading) in the development of European integration and the switch towards a new centre of policy-making.

This approach was partly identified by Featherstone and Kazamias (2001) when they considered that domestic structures were not the passive recipients of EU impacts. 'Domestic and EU institutional settings are intermeshed, with actors engaged in both vertical and horizontal networks and institutional linkages' (p. 1). They emphasized changes brought about on domestic policy in terms of fit or misfit and how the member states deal with these. 'Europeanization is assumed to be a two way process, between the domestic and the EU levels, involving both top-down and bottom-up pressures' (ibid., p. 6). The success in negotiations between domestic actors at the EU level will determine the level of fit or misfit when it comes to policy implementation. 'An effective strategy of maximizing the benefits and minimizing the costs of European policies is to "up-load" national policies to the European level and shape EU policies accordingly' (Börzel, 2003, p. 4).

The level of success regarding uploading (En2) will determine the level of change in relation to downloading (En1). It could be argued, that if there has been no misfit at the domestic level, if change has failed to occur, Europeanization has not taken place. This is when it is important to investigate bottom-up aspects of Europeanization and identify the levels of success in member state uploading. If member states have lobbied effectively and had much of their perspective included in EU policy, misfit will be limited and consequent domestic change will be minimal. This does not mean that Europeanization has not taken place but that En2 was effective and En1 minimized. 'Member states are not merely the passive takers of European demands for domestic change. They may proactively shape European policies, institutions and processes to which they have to adapt later...Moreover, the need to adapt domestically to European pressures may have significant effects at the European level, where member states seek to reduce "misfit" between European and domestic arrangements by shaping EU decisions' (Börzel, 2003, p. 3). Furthermore, Börzel (2003) notes that the interaction between these dimensions may be investigated through the actions of national governments. Arguments developed in this text agree with this position, but considers the supranational dimension as the domain of European integration and that uploading is not simply undertaken at the national or macro level but that sub-national actors are also involved in micro uploading (En2). Fundamentally, it perceives uploading in terms of macro (national) and micro (sub-national) activities. Indeed, there is a distinction between intergovernmental and neo-functional perspectives of uploading which will be covered in more detail below.

'Content' elements of Europeanization incorporate policy transfer as identified by Bomberg and Peterson (2000) and shared beliefs, identified by Radealli (2000) and Olsen (2002). There are also nuances regarding content in terms of different variables, for instance an interpretation of Europeanization relating to policy transfer would need to identify when policy transfer was horizontal and when it was vertical. Vertical policy transfer comes through EU policy or European integration processes. Horizontal policy transfer incorporates learning from and taking on other member state policies without EU involvement. This provides a parameter for Europeanization and deals with 'conceptual stretching' in that if an occurrence of policy transfer is to be perceived as Europeanization it needs to come through EU institutions even if this only incorporates co-ordination. However, the level of co-ordination or activity when distinguishing between horizontal and vertical policy transfer is debatable.

When we investigate crossloading (En3) and its links with policy transfer as noted two forms of policy transfer can be identified: vertical and horizontal policy transfer. Horizontal policy transfer may never involve Europeanization. However when it does it is less explicitly En3 because policy has not been through the European integration process and policy transfer is undertaken from one state to another. However, policies that are transferred in this fashion may become the norm throughout the EU and are consequently macro or micro uploaded into the EU domain. Policy outcomes through interaction between En2 and European integration are eventually downloaded to domestic domains where again cultural interpretations take place which could trigger the basis of further En3. Vertical policy transfer is more overtly En3 because it has been through EU institutions. Vertical policy transfer is where one domestic interpretation of En1 supersedes another. Again this can intensify and become the basis for further macro or micro En2. The dominant policy may be uploaded and following European integration, downloaded to the membership. Again differences in interpretation will occur however, with vertical policy transfer, levels of diversity will decrease. Indeed the process can be formulated in the following way:

Horizontal policy transfer (HPT)
Vertical policy transfer (VPT)
European integration (EI)
Downloading (En1)
Uploading (En2)
Crossloading (En3)

HPT = impetus for policy change can begin in this way but would not ordinarily have been through supranational structures.

HPT – En2 – EI – En1 – VPT/En3

VPT = impetus for policy is likely to be an outcome of En2, EI and En1.

En2 – EI – En1 – VPT/En3

But may again precipitate further uploading through the formation of shared beliefs.

VPT/En3 – En2 – EI – En1

In most policy domains HPT could be seen as the trigger for change and may only occur during the initial phase of policy transfer in the EU. In this context, once convergence has been kick-started and the process begun then the outcomes of En1 would be VPT/En3. Unless a sector or government saw deficiencies in the policy issue and successfully transferred changes through HPT to other member states which were then uploaded and downloaded. Again however, it is likely that any further Europeanization regarding this issue would involve VPT/En3. Consequently, this study will identify En3 as VPT, because for Europeanization to take place policy necessitates an explicit EU dimension. In this way Europeanization can be seen as En1, En2 and En3 (see Figure 3.1).

Shared beliefs may be observed in the creation of the Single European Market (SEM) where diverse beliefs relating to the market are streamlined under one regulatory structure. However, even though differing interpretations of regulation re-emerge at the

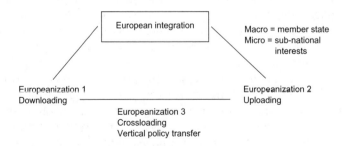

Figure 3.1 Europeanization and European integration

domestic level certain beliefs have been shared, for example, liberal market structures in the SEM (Howell, 1999, 2000, this is covered in Chapter 7 below). Of course, member states attempt to upload domestic beliefs but at some point through political expediency or necessity these become compromised and start to form shared beliefs. The 'content' of Europeanization includes numerous ideas such as institutional norms (accountability), informal rules (democracy), discourse (language used when discussing issues relating to the EU e.g. EMU) and identities (e.g. does the euro provide an EU identity?). Indeed, content in many instances revolves around accepted ideas regarding the civil constitution and is based on areas of recognition.

If as substantive theories En1, En2 or En3 are examined individually they are easier to subject to empirical analysis than when they are mixed or incorporate elements of 'content'. For example, when investigating identities and how these may have been affected by Europeanization a number of different variables can be observed in terms of localization, regionalization and globalization that make the effects of En1, En2 and En3 difficult to determine. The same may be said of shared beliefs however, even though variables here are difficult to disentangle, one is able to identify shared beliefs in the compromised regulatory structures of the SEM. However, the clearest examples of Europeanization may be found through analysis of structures and policies and the part the EU plays in 'diffusion and construction' (Radealli, 2000) or downloading and uploading.

Europeanization is conceptualized as substantive theories in the context of 'situation' in terms of downloading (En1), uploading (En2) and crossloading (En3) (see Figure 3.1). Each of these conceptualizations allows situations where empirical reliability can be made explicit from a particular perspective. Each individually relies on a positivist methodology where phenomena can be broken down into independent and dependent variables and provide an analysis and explanation of thin causal effects. However, if a primarily positivist perspective is undertaken 'we lose sight of the complex, interwoven interdependent relationship between strategy and discursive construction of the constraints and opportunities' involved in the process of European integration (Dyson, 2000, p. 647). If the study is to ensure an all round understanding of the affects of Europeanization on the EU and member states an analysis needs to include En1, En2, En3 and instances of content. To provide empirical reliability and validity and the 'interwoven relationships' at work in the EU, Europeanization needs to identify aspects of 'fit' and 'misfit' and see the interaction between En1, En2 and En3 as an example of 'process'. In such a way elements of constructivism are brought into the analysis where the variables are changeable and findings created as investigation proceeds.

Through bringing together different aspects of Europeanization we are not simply pursuing theory testing but 'organising concepts', 'selecting relevant facts' and constructing narrative as well as ensuring levels of empirical reliability (George, 1976). This moves the study away from 'thin causal effects' towards thicker understandings and perspectives of processes at work in the EU (Dyson, 2000). Europeanization as 'process' can be identified as meso theory that provides an analytical basis for multilevel governance through drawing on aspects of grand theory. On the other hand En1, En2 and En3 as examples of situation may be seen as substantive theories or models in the context of proximity to data, idealizing and simplification. The greater the simplification, the more likely theory will be open to positivist procedures – the more complicated the theory, the better it is able to develop a constructivist understanding of phenomenon. Simplification allows clear indications of cause and effect as well as idealized prediction. Complication enables depth of understanding regarding process; fundamentally the two can be used together to provide both theoretical explanation and understanding of empirical phenomenon (see Figure 3.2).

In the context of En1, Radaelli (2000) identified four ways by which member states respond to EU changes. First he considers 'accommodation' in which downloading is compatible with domestic structures, policies, discourses and identities; second, 'transformation' where downloading poses a challenge to these areas; third is 'inertia', which is when a political will to bring about change does not exist. Fourth, he identifies 'retrenchment', this is when a downloaded policy area

Positivism	Constructivism
En1, En2, En3	En1/En2/En3/EI/Content

Figure 3.2 Methodological mix

strengthens opposition to the EU and provides an impetus for anti-European interests and dismantling aspects of European integration. The problem with these definitions is that they only deal with downloading and fail to identify how elements of uploading and the European integration process may have an impact on the acceptability of EU policy and so affect 'accommodation', 'transformation', 'inertia' or 'retrenchment'.

Olsen (2002) identified Europeanization as the changes taking place in member states and then outlines processes of institutional change that may indicate how/why it takes place. However, even though he indicates separate interpretations of Europeanization, the different conceptualizations are inclusive rather than exclusive. In his paper Olsen separates Europeanization into five possible phenomena when examining what is actually changing and considers that it may be seen as:

(a) Changes in external territorial boundaries;
(b) Governance institutions developed at the supranational level;
(c) Influencing and imposing supranationality at the sub-national and national levels;
(d) Exporting governance procedure and policy specific for EU beyond EU borders;
(e) A project of a political nature aimed at intensifying the unification of the EU.

There are a number of issues regarding these proposed elements of Europeanization. Changes to external borders or Enlargement incorporates change in the domestic policies of those joining the EU and existing members who will change policy to take this extension into account. In this context, accession states undergo En1 and En3 prior to EU membership and EU governance procedures are exported beyond EU borders. Accession states have been open to En1 and En3 without participation in En2 or European integration processes. This is investigated in relation to Poland in Part III.

Developed governance institutions at the supranational level indicate European integration; however the development of the EU policy-making institutions incorporates uploading and bottom-up Europeanization (En2). This creates a slight problem because the development of EU policy-making institutions is continual so to deal with the interaction between Europeanization and European integration one needs to take a snapshot from a bottom-up perspective. The same may be said of the changes to the domestic level through the imposition of supranationality on sub-national and national levels. This may be identified as the top-down effects of Europeanization (En1) on both member and non-member states; there is an interaction between European integration and Europeanization and the need to provide a snapshot from a top-down and/or bottom-up perspectives. However, to provide a full understanding of the EU each snapshot will need to take into consideration aspects of the other as well as the interactions between En1, En2, En3 and European integration. As noted, differentiation in levels of policy-making had been identified through multilevel governance however, this only dealt with 'situation' and led to accusations of description. This study attempts to add to multilevel governance by identifying 'process' and interaction between the levels. This is achieved by identifying different aspects of Europeanization in relation to European integration and deconstructing neo-functionalism and intergovernmentalism in terms of state preferences, sub-national interests, supranationality and spillover.

Europeanization and European integration: re-assessing grand European integration theory

In addition to difficulties with Europeanization we also encounter conceptual problems regarding European integration. For instance, in some definitions it is difficult to distinguish between Europeanization and European integration and in others they seem to be identical. In this context, why bother with the notion of Europeanization? Why not simply carry on with the well worn but tried and tested idea of European integration?

As noted above, Olsen (2002) concluded that the EU was a political project (in the context of unification) and it is in this way that European integration and Europeanization could be seen as one and the same thing. To assess the relationship between Europeanization and European integration grand theories needed to be investigated. Indeed, it is through this investigation that deficiencies with Europeanization and European integration theory may be overcome. Through a re-assessment of neo-functionalism and intergovernmentalism we may comprehend better the differences and similarities between European integration and Europeanization and how both may extend our comprehension of European integration. Consequently, by breaking down Europeanization into substantive theory in terms of En1, En2, En3, European integration and 'content' we may make better use of the meso theory in relation to neo-functionalism and intergovernmentalism or grand theory. This may provide the basis for verification and generalization regarding certain aspects of neo-functionalism but also allows for areas, which are more difficult to empirically verify to also undergo investigation. In such a way aspects of positivism and constructivism may be brought together in an analysis of the EU.

Problems with European integration theory in general arose as the explanatory power of neo-functionalism was criticized. The main 'weakness of neo-functionalism was not empirical but theoretical ... once the simple teleology toward integration was abandoned neo-functionalism and other grand theories lacked the resources to construct a positive response. Neofunctionalists ... concluded that an explanation of integration must be embedded in a multicausal framework comprised of narrower theories' (Moravcsik, 1998, p. 14). However, as George (1976) indicated the 'important question is why?' He suggests that the reason had less to do with what was happening in the EU and more to do with a change in values and interpretations of reality and theory in the United States and 'that the doubts expressed about neo-functionalism were a reflection of the doubts expressed about the techno-managerial society' (p. 33) and difficulties relating to positivist prediction. Indeed, at the same time as neo-functionalism was under scrutiny unified theories in the United States were also undergoing critical examination where theories such as structural functionalism were perceived as too abstract to 'permit concrete theory testing' (Moravcsik, 1998, p. 33). Europeanization as a meso theory provides the opportunity to break down neo-functionalism and intergovernmentalism in such a way to allow a modicum of empirical reliability. For instance, aspects of Europeanization such as downloading or uploading may be empirically investigated and verified or negated. Furthermore, as noted above, intergovernmentalism was criticized because the notion of national preference did not take into consideration the numerous interests that make up this preference. Indeed, it has been suggested that a concentration on the Council of Ministers was too narrow.

Europeanization may be interpreted as a means of overcoming some of the criticisms levelled at intergovernmentalism and neo-functionalism. For instance, functional spillover (or task expansion) may be understood in terms of top-down Europeanization and the interpretation of the legislation downloaded from the EU as aspects of intergovernmentalism. This allows an understanding of the distinction between integrative legislation provided by the EU and diverse domestic interpretations brought about through Europeanization. European integration may be understood as the outcome of domestic uploading to the EU level through Europeanization as well as the process of downloading once an accepted compromise has been reached. Through uploading and cultivated spillover, EU diversity is integrated through shared beliefs; however, when downloading comes into operation each member state will interpret policies based on their own cultural perspective. Integration does take place, but not to the extent that EU policy originally envisaged. Furthermore, for En3 to occur transferral should go through the EU and involve some form of cultivated spillover. Uploading may be conceived in either macro terms where national preferences may be uploaded by member state governments through the Council of Ministers, Corepers or Inter-Governmental Conferences (IGCs), or micro terms, where industry and sector preferences are uploaded through interest groups. Macro uploading is closely linked with intergovernmental perspectives and micro uploading with neo-functionalism.

Europeanization indicates a continual interaction or dialectic between the uniformity of the EU and the diversity of the individual member states. An explicit example of this can be found in Bulmer and Burch (2000) where they provide a study of the Europeanization of central government. They argued that changes to UK and German central governments have occurred but that these have been incremental rather than radical. Transformation has taken place but diversity is still apparent. Consequently there is no end-state because, as the EU develops, member state diversity is in a continual state of flux. This has implications for one of the main criticisms of neo-functionalism or its teleology and negates theory as a means of predicting outcomes.

Europeanization and European integration continuously interact with each other; for instance the development of the supranational level can be seen as bottom-up (En2) Europeanization, in the context of institutions and policy. Bottom-up Europeanization (En2) indicates the use of sub-national interests in the development of European integration, the switch towards a new centre of policy-making and the proactive role the Commission plays in this process. The existence of the new centre of policy-making (supranational institutions or policies themselves) indicates European integration, with the implementation of policies through supranational institutions incorporating top-down Europeanization (En1). Overall, the EU environment encompasses European integration and uploading, downloading and crossloading incorporate Europeanization. On the one hand, Europeanization can be seen as the source of change in relation to the EU level in terms of European integration and the development of supranationality. On the other hand, European integration can be seen as the source of change and Europeanization the outcome of change on member state governmental, legal and regulatory structures. Overall, we have interactions between Europeanization and European integration as well as three aspects of spillover in the construction and perpetuation of supranational institutions and development of EU and domestic policies and systems. As noted in the previous chapter, multilevel governance is apparent in EU policy-making procedures. Europeanization identifies the interactions between these levels and makes these explicit when it draws on aspects of grand theory.

Conclusion

This chapter overviewed a number of problems relating to conceptualizations of Europeanization and outlined the difference between Europeanization and European integration. The problem of 'conceptual stretching' was discussed and the chapter argued that it was necessary to draw boundaries around Europeanization. It attempts this by breaking down Europeanization into three substantive theories relating to 'situation' and 'process' (En1, En2 and En3) and 'content'. The more content indicated the more complications when attempting to determine the strength and empirical reliability of positivist explanations of EU and domestic environments.

Europeanization can be understood from an En2 (bottom-up) or En1 (top-down) perspective, European integration comprises the environment on which Europeanization impacts or from which it emanates. However, it is more complicated than this with interaction between the two areas merging into one another for different lengths of time and at differing levels of intensity. This means that at different times the emphasis on Europeanization will either be based around mechanisms of change in terms of uploading from the domestic to the EU level, downloading from the EU to the domestic level or crossloading through policy transfer. Indeed, the success of the member state in terms of uploading will have implications when it comes to downloading in respect of impacts and change on the domestic environment. The success in uploading will affect misfit and consequently have an impact on downloading in the context of fit. Furthermore, through crossloading different interpretations of policy mechanisms may be overcome and in some instances bring about further En2 and European integration. One may argue that this is why in most instances En1, En2 and En3 as well as European integration procedures need to be brought into the equation and a constructivist as well as positivist perspective incorporated.

Conceptually, there are differences between Europeanization and European integration but there is also a dialogic and dialectical process between the two that is seamless. In dealing with this paradox the chapter moves away from a purely positivist perspective and mechanisms like dependent and independent variables. Reality and theory are not external to social existence but, with a continual flux between variables, constructed by human beings in historical situations. Consequently, theory should reflect this flux and rather than mirror some external reality in a precise manner or predict, acknowledge transactional dialectical change. There should be empirical reliability and generalization but theory should also reflect the intricacies of the process. Europeanization is made up of En1, En2 and En3, which incorporate the outcomes and in-puts of European integration, as well as identify the interaction between these elements through 'content' fit/misfit and impacts.

Even though En1 provides the opportunity for clear empirical reliability and some validity it fails to fully explain the interactions at work in the process of European integration. A deeper mix of methodologies is necessary and the interactions between En1, En2 and En3 might be made more explicit. However, it is at this point that limitations need to be drawn around the concept, otherwise it is too broad and we revert to a grand theory, limited reliability and 'conceptual stretching'. Indeed, this demarcation allows certain elements of neo-functionalism, that is, sub-national interests, spillover and supranationality, to undergo empirical examination with a full comprehension of the interactions involved in the process of European integration.

En1, En2 and En3 are conceptualizations of Europeanization, which incorporate change at the EU level and the outcomes of change at the domestic level, with emphasis placed on the interaction between European integration and Europeanization as 'process'. En1, En2 and En3 allow a mix of methodology in the context of positivism and constructivism. 'Content' indicates more inclusive conceptualizations of Europeanization that lean towards a constructivist methodological approach. This means they are more difficult to submit to reliable empirical analysis and allow criticisms of 'conceptual stretching'. The mix of methodologies apparent in amalgamations of En1, En2 and En3 provide 'thicker data' and a more precise understanding as well as explanation of the EU and the 'process' of European integration. However, if a study wished to undertake a more positivist investigation, then concentration on situation in terms of En1, En2 or En3 (substantive theory) would be conducive to this approach. When En1, En2 and En3 are mixed and we start to identify 'process', the study begins to mix methodologies; the greater the mix/synthesis, the more emphasis will be placed on constructivism.

In general this part has been concerned with issues relating to theoretical and empirical discussions regarding the conceptual nature of Europeanization and European integration. The philosophical ideas of Kant and Hegel provide the basis for realism and functionalism, which European integration theory and Europeanization draw on when explaining European integration processes and changes in member states. The next part deals with historical issues regarding European integration and Europeanization and identifies how in the initial stages European integration theory adequately explained European integration processes. In the latter stages (following the Luxembourg compromise and later the SEA) grand theory became questionable in positivist terms and more precise theory was required. Initial attempts to provide this involved multilevel governance and state-centric approaches; later attempts incorporated institutionalism and Europeanization. Part III concentrates on empirical instances of European integration and Europeanization. It concentrates on EU financial services regulation in terms of banking, investment and insurance directives, domestic competent authorities and the Financial Services Action Plan (FSAP).

Part II

Europeanization and European Integration: A Historical Perspective

Introduction

This part identifies the distinction between explanations of the European Union (EU) in its initial stages during the 1950s and 1960s, during a period of stagnation over the 1970s and rejuvenation during the 1980s and 1990s. In the 1950s neo-functionalism best explained European integration processes whereas in the 1960s and 1970s there was a shift towards intergovernmentalism. However, in the 1980s and 1990s neither grand theory completely explained the process, which led to the development of meso theories in terms of multilevel governance, state-centricism and Europeanization. This study considers that Europeanization provides a more succinct explanation of the EU and in an empirical context identified the distinction between neo-functionalism and intergovernmentalism.

Kantian and Hegelian perspectives as well as grand theories are discussed in relation to the historical process in the provision of a theoretical framework. The broader perspectives are not discarded but used to give insight into the arguments forwarded by those involved in the development of the EU. In the second phase of European integration, Europeanization is able to further clarify a number of issues raised in the initial phase in terms of supranational institutions, spillover and sub-national interests. Indeed, the final chapter in this part discusses sub-national interests as micro uploaders and examines their role in the development of the EU. Issues relating to sub-national interests, supranational institutions, spillover and member state preferences are discussed in more detail in Part III.

Overall, macro uploading in relation to member state preferences and European integration are investigated in relation to micro uploading and sub-national interests. Downloading is also touched upon in terms of functional spillover and member state interpretation of directives and regulations. Paradoxically, integrated policies downloaded from the EU providing diverse interpretation and domestic cultural distinction.

4

Europeanization and European Integration: Empirical and Historical Developments

Introduction

In this chapter we turn to more empirical matters and the occurrences that impacted on the formation of the EU. This is not to say that ideas and actions are divorced from each other but that the two areas continually interact in the formation of phenomenon. In 1945, most agreed that the Wilsonian agreement that followed the First World War was flawed and in the aftermath of the Second World War a different form of treaty was necessary. Many considered that the Versailles Treaty precipitated and ensured the outbreak of the Second World War and, if a lasting peace was to be realized in Europe, new strategies needed to be explored. 'In 1919 Germany's first democratic government was forced to its knees with ... an impossible settlement and so was left open to be vilified by the lurking reaction as traitors to the nations life and honour' (Mitrany, 1975c, p. 19). Indeed, it has been argued that in the immediate post-Second World War period many wanted to replace the European system of nation-states with a new polity of European citizenship (Pinder, 1993). However, in the aftermath of the Second World War, this was not the only rationale for the formation of the EU. The Cold War was also perceived as a reason for constructing a united Europe so it could act as a defence buffer against the Soviet Union. Hobsbawm (1995) argued that the main emphasis for the creation of the 'European Community' was the Cold War. It was 'an entirely unprecedented form of political organization, namely a permanent (or at least long lasting) arrangement to integrate the economies, and to some extent legal systems, of a number of independent nation-states' (p. 239). However, following the Cold War the EU continued to thrive as membership expanded 'and was in theory committed to even closer political, as well as economic integration. This was to lead to permanent federal or con-federal political union for "Europe" ' (ibid., p. 240). An integrated Europe was not simply about dealing with external factors but a means of overcoming internal problems that had materialized in two world wars. Of course, between the evolving membership there were differences regarding the levels of integration with member states, at different historical moments, clamouring for greater or less political and economic integration.

Carr (1993) argued, that before the First World War when partici-pating in wars, Britain had perceived itself as fighting for the freedom of Europe and humanity (cited in Williams *et al.*, 1993, p. 183). Indeed, realists argued that states formulated policy preference in relation to the national interest. However, as noted 'British national interests in the post-war world tended to be defined in rather broader terms than were the national interests of some other west European states, reflecting the legacy of Britain's role as the dominant state in the international system of the nineteenth century and its status as an imperial power' (George, 1998, p. 12). Such sentiments underpin some of the Eurosceptic arguments in the United Kingdom against monetary union and the development of a EU constitution in the early twenty-first century. This chapter investigates the historical rationales for these differences in both the United Kingdom and other member states and how these impact on the formation of common markets and monetary union.

An integrated Europe? A practical endeavour

During the inter-war years intellectuals, academics and politicians were involved in debates regarding the future structure of Europe. In the 1920s a pan-European movement proposal (made by Coudenhove-Kalergi an Austrian aristocrat) won the support of Briand and Stresseman, the French and German foreign ministers, who con-sidered that the idea of a united Europe was a means of preventing fur-ther war. The movement lacked a mass following and appealed mostly to diplomats and intellectuals and had a very hazy idea of what a

European federation would entail; this incoherency and the victory of national-socialism in Germany put paid to the Briand–Stresseman plan in particular and the pan-European movement in general. The extent of support for integration is still a major problem today. In the United Kingdom, there have been calls for Economic and Monetary Union (EMU) and further integration. However, there are those who consider that when the United Kingdom joined the European Economic Community (EEC) in 1973, this was all it joined, and that any further participation should be approved through another referendum. The two models that are usually posited when identifying levels of involvement in the EU are the billiard ball and spider-web approaches. The former perceives Europe as a family of nation-states dealing with one another for required durations on specific issues (where the balls touch for as long as is necessary); the latter pictures a situation in which member states become more and more linked to one another in all aspects of polity and policy-making. Altiero Spinnelli (an Italian MEP) could be considered a proponent of the latter and Winston Churchill of the former. The former approach is close to an intergovernmental or con-federal perspective and the latter federal or neo-functional. However, at some point and for different reasons both saw the rationale of a united Europe. Spinnelli described how a group of intellectuals imprisoned by Mussolini envisaged a post-war Europe in which a European authority would take over national defence foreign policy and economic affairs because they considered national authorities had failed so badly.

At the start of the Second World War Churchill proposed an Anglo-French army, a single parliament and full union between the two powers. One may argue that the proposals of a union between the two countries were dictated by the difficult situation facing Europe. The proposal took the French by surprise and their subsequent refusal saw the end of federal activity in Britain. In the end, German victory in France put an end to such ideas. Britain found herself alone and facing a difficult time in her history and during this period one may posit two expressions of British consciousness. The first involved a united loyalty of British citizens against a common enemy. Public opinion had to be loyal to the nation because the whole nation counted on this loyalty. The second involved a loss of faith with Europe and any ideas of integration being replaced with minimal confidence in mainland European states. These expressions of consciousness were further intensified through the different war-time experiences of member states. Most of Europe condemned the part nationalism played in the creation of National-Socialism and fascism. Most saw the nation–state as the institution that underpinned these movements. However, for Britain the nation-state provided the basis of victory and the liberation of Europe and may illustrate the differences of opinion between the member states regarding the extent of European integration.

In general, the peoples of the Europe condemned the part that nationalism had played in the rise of fascism and a pledge was taken by a number of European governments to create a European union designed to prevent the future outbreak of war. The First European Federalist Congress (EFC) met in Paris in March 1945 and decided 'to promote the federal organisation of the European peoples'.

The architects of the European Coal and Steel Community (ECSC) and the EEC were deeply influenced by the sentiments outlined by the EFC and none more so than the chief architect Jean Monnet. Monnet argued that European unity could be achieved through the creation of specialized administrative bodies at the European level, which, by carrying out specific functions, would attract political authority to themselves, and away from national governments. Effectively, he posited a functional approach to integration. As noted in Chapter 2, Monnet and Schuman perceived a Europe based on functional institutions and evolving integration.

In 1946, Winston Churchill also recognized the need for a joint conduct of affairs when he called for 'a kind of United States of Europe'. However, as indicated above, what kind of Europe Churchill envisaged was based on the lines of intergovernmentalism or in substantive terms the billiard ball model, but this did not stop Edward Heath celebrating the fiftieth anniversary of Churchill's speech in 1996 with a call for closer integration.

In May 1948, the Congress of Europe initiated the formulation of the Council of Europe and this became active in May 1949. The Council was based on economic and political union with an emphasis on a European assembly. Article 1 of the statute stated, 'The aim of the Council of Europe is to achieve a greater unity between its Members for the purposes of safeguarding and realising the ideals and principles which are their common heritage and facilitating their economic and social progress' (cited in Nugent, 1999, pp. 15–16).

Pro-integrationists hoped this would be the first step towards greater European integration. However, they were to be disappointed. The Council involved no surrender of national sovereignty; decisions were only taken if unanimity prevailed and its members were drawn from national legislatures. Such proved to be too weak to create an impetus for European integration. The Council of Europe continues to perform useful functions, most notably in the field of human rights and as a forum for discussing common interests. But there are 21 members in this and it is intergovernmental in the extreme and best represented by the billiard ball model.

European Union: peaceful co-operation and economic reconstruction

During the 1920s, it had been taken for granted that any form of a united Europe would stretch from the Urals to the Atlantic: consequently, in 1945 many still perceived and hoped for such a union. However, due to the Cold War and later British reluctance, such was not to be the case. Europe had been devastated by the war and the need to re-build was imperative. The problem was that products to ensure reconstruction were in short supply and many of those that were produced were exported to the United States.

A war agency to investigate post-war reconstruction was set up in 1943, which was superseded in 1947 by the United Nations Economic Committee (UNEC). However, even at this early date co-operation between the West and the USSR was deteriorating. The USSR was looking for both reparations and security and this was souring relations with the United States. By 1946, the USSR was dominant in Eastern Europe and in response to this the United States launched the Marshall Plan (1947). In the post-war period, until 1989, Cold War as well as periods of détente ensured that economic co-operation was confined to 16 Western European states. This was subsequently institutionalized in June 1948 through the Organization for European Economic Co-operation (OEEC). The OEEC was set up to administer the Marshall Plan, assist European economic recovery, encourage the abolition of tariffs and ultimately develop into a permanent organization for West European co-operation. However, the Marshall Plan and the OEEC were not seen as adequate for dealing with the internal problems that plagued Europe during the post-war period and beyond. The Marshall Plan enabled economic reconstruction in the face of external threats but failed to deal with peaceful co-operation and internal threats. Consequently, in 1950 the need for functional institutions which would bring together both political and economic variables in the quest for closer European integration were proposed by Jean Monnet and Robert Schuman.

Perpetual peace and civil constitution: the European Coal and Steel Community

Jean Monnet and Robert Schuman, who have been described as the founding fathers of the EU, instigated a plan to allow the foundations of a unified Europe. Primarily, their plan was to underpin Franco-German reconciliation through pooling the production of two strategically important industries, coal and steel. 'Undoubtedly, a major reason for the initiative was French concern at the possible threat to French interests posed by the steady post-war increase in German productivity' (Linter and Mazey, 1991, p. 4). Effectively, the ECSC was a means of controlling the products needed to perpetuate war. There was both a political and economic objective to it: peaceful co-operation and the generation of economies of scale to aid the recovery process.

Monnet and Schuman perceived long-term political objectives in the gradual evolution of the EU, from economic integration to political union. The responsibilities of ECSC were limited to those two commodities (coal and steel), which were still part of the member states' general economies.

> The pooling of coal and steel production should immediately provide for the setting up of common foundations for economic development as a first step in the federation of Europe and will change the destinies of those regions which have long been devoted to the manufacture of munitions for war, of which they have been the most constant victims. The solidarity in production thus established will make it plain that any war between France and Germany becomes not merely unthinkable, but materially impossible. The setting up of this powerful productive unit, open to all countries ... will lay a true foundation for their economic unification.
> (Schuman, 1950, cited in Stirk and Weigal, 1999, p. 76)

The basis of the ECSC, the Treaty of Paris, incorporated a different type of treaty. It was one that, as pointed out by Kant (1995b), involved no secret reservation for a future war. It was the basis of the Kantian civil constitution (Kant, 1995a). Indeed, it is not only the ECSC that ensured European countries did not fight each other but that they did not want to enter into conflict. 'Nevertheless, the Coal and Steel Authority, the Common Market, the Common Foreign and Security Policy and Common Agricultural Policy ... have performed reinforcing functions. They have introduced a new degree of openness hitherto unknown in Europe' (Cooper, 2003, p. 35). The ECSC ensured transparency, in that it involved an institution with a particular function that went beyond the member state in terms of openness, the generation of economies of scale and reinforced peaceful co-operation. However the ECSC was not an international institution and incorporated a structure on which Haas (1958) based his concepts of supranationalism and neo-functionalism.

In 1950 the United Kingdom was invited to join the ECSC, however there was some concern regarding the attitude of trade unions to the proposal and although the government was not opposed to the ECSC, in principle, they could not accept a supranational authority or a cartel like restrictive model. The government felt that they should discuss the issue in detail because although the ECSC was likely to go ahead, discussions in Paris were likely to hold the project up for some time. 'The greatest risk was perhaps that deadlock would be reached in those discussions and the United Kingdom Government would be asked to resolve it' (Documents on British Policies Overseas, Series 2, Vol. 1 pp. 210–13 cited in Stirk and Weigall, 1999, pp. 81–2). This attitude illustrates the imperialistic perspective the United Kingdom had of European politics in the post-Second World War period and one which still exists in certain circles today. British interests were global, it was an international power which when required, will resolve disputes between other European states. Of course, things will not work without the United Kingdom so we have the time to inspect new proposals in detail and if they are achieved remain on the side-lines until we are sure these new institutions work. This perspective is based on the United Kingdom's imperialist past and can be observed not only in attitudes towards the ECSC but towards the EEC and EMU as well. This could be interpreted as incorporating simply a subjective perspective of self-identity rather than the inclusive recognition expressed by the six founding member states. However, it soon became clear in the early 1950s and 1960s that, especially with regard to France, this objective/subjective recognition was rather limited.

Whereas the UK Government was dragging its feet, Jean Monnet argued that larger markets were necessary because prosperity would prove difficult, if not impossible, unless the states of Europe formed themselves into a federation or a European entity, which would engender a common economic unit. During the war, Monnet was appointed as de Gaulle's representative in Anglo-American economic negotiations. While in the United States, Monnet encountered American economic planning and market-size, which convinced him that in a post-war Europe tariff barriers and frontiers should be abolished.

Economists noted the differences between US and European economic growth during the inter-war years. Between 1900 and 1938 US output had increased by 163 per cent. In 1913 Western Europe produced about 50 per cent of the world's industrial goods, but by 1953 it produced approximately 25 per cent and had been overtaken by the United States. Economists argued that the reason for this was that larger markets led to economies of greater scale whereby mass production and better distribution allowed lower production costs. Large-scale producers had easier access to sources of capital and wider competition, which stimulated both technical improvements and plant modernization. What seemed to exemplify this had been the success of Ford, Rockefeller and Carnegie in the early twentieth century. Monnet was among those who contended that, in a post-war situation, the introduction of modern financial organizations and new technology from the United States would lead to the creation of larger industrial units and groupings. Furthermore, two world wars had not helped productivity and in this context the links between economic prosperity and peaceful co-operation were made explicit. Perpetual peace provided the basis for economic prosperity, which in itself enhanced trade and the consequent recognition.

In 1946, Monnet was given the task of modernizing and re-equipping French industry, so he established the *Commisariat au Plan*. This encompassed planned production according to the needs of the country in major areas of the French economy, that is, coal, steel, electricity and transport. However, by the late 1940s it was evident that economies of scale were difficult to achieve at a national level and that in a post-Second World War world, cross-border planning was essential. At the time of ratification it was made clear by pro-integrationists that, the ECSC was only a breach in the wall of national sovereignty and unless further integration was enacted, the breach would close again. However, an attempt to 'establish a Political Community based on integrated defence forces was defeated in 1954 by a combination of nationalists and Stalinists in the French National Assembly, it became clear that a direct assault on national sovereignty was unlikely to succeed' (Pinder, 1995, p. 51). Functional approaches were difficult to achieve in the face of realist and intergovernmental perspectives. However, as noted by Kant (1995b), the civil constitution would be realized through learning from previous mistakes, antagonisms would be reconciled through shared objectives and the recognition of self and other in the pursuit of these objectives.

European Defence Community (EDC) and European Political Community (EPC)

In the early 1950s the United States began to supply military aid to Europe and called for the re-arming of Germany. They considered that without German military power the defence of Europe would be impossible. Furthermore, 'there was another institutional development in the 1950s... the projected European Defence Community (EDC)' (Nugent, 1999, p. 42). The French called for a European army (this was out of the fear of a resurrected German army). 'The French Government have now produced a proposal for a European army with a European Minister of Defence. This European army would contain German units as well as units from other countries... His Majesty's Government do not favour this proposal... We cherish our special ties with our old European friends, but in our view, Europe is not enough; it is not big enough, it is not strong enough to stand alone' (Bevin, E., November 1950; House of Commons Debates, Hansard Vol. 481, Cols 1172–4 cited in Stirk and Weigall, 1999, p. 109). Consequently, when the conference met to discuss the EDC the only states present were the members of the ECSC. Furthermore, Article 38 of the proposed EDC provided an embryonic European Political Community (EPC). The structure of the EDC would have been similar to the ECSC. Indeed, these were to be structured on neo-functional lines and incorporated supranational institutions that dealt with foreign policy and defence. However, the EDC and the EPC failed to gain ratification for a number of reasons which involved: the end of the Korean War, the death of Stalin and the unwillingness of member states, especially France, to relinquish sovereignty in the political domain. The early 1950s saw the end of the period that was favourable towards European Union. Effectively, this period witnessed the failure of neo-functional or supranational policy-making in areas of high politics. However, the ECSC succeeded and from this the EEC and Euratom were to emerge.

In June 1955 foreign ministers of the six member states of the ECSC met at Messina where the following resolution was agreed. 'The governments of (the six)...consider that the moment has arrived to initiate a new phase on the path of constructing Europe' (cited in Hodges, 1972, p. 67). Even though there had been problems with the EPC and EDC elements of neo-functionalism seemed to explain the ongoing development of the EU and 'ever closer union'. However, aspects of intergovernmentalism were apparent in that member states, as they had been with the ECSC, were involved in the development of the EEC and Euratom. 'Recognition' and 'civil constitution' were expanded through macro uploading and European integration in the form of new communities.

In April 1956, the Spaak report was accepted and used as the basis of negotiations that in 1957 produced both the Euratom and EEC treaties. Of the two, the EEC was by far the most important and built on the sentiments outlined in the Messina resolution. 'The Messina Conference of 1955 marks the moment when the European movement turned to economic integration as the leading edge in its strategy. The political strand was not making progress; members decided that a strong and successful economic community would open up the surest path for pursuing their long term political goals' (Davies, 1997, pp. 1085–6). Article 2 of the EEC treaty identifies the objectives of the EEC, which 'shall have as its task, by establishing a common market and progressively approximating the economic policies of Member States, to promote throughout the community a harmonious development of economic activities, a continuous and balanced expansion, an increase in stability, an accelerated raising of the standards of living and closer relations of the states belonging to it' (Treaties of Rome HMSO, 1988, Art. 2).

Through the intergovernmental/neo-functional initiation of the ECSC and eventually the EEC, the neo-functional approach to European integration was formalized. Functionalism already looked towards pursuing internationalism through communication and technocrats. However, the use of sector integration provided the processes to be used at the European level. Functionalism led Haas and Lindberg to the concept of neo-functionalism, which incorporated integration through incremental steps, supranational institutions and technocratic groupings at the regional level. 'The piecemeal approach to European integration adopted by Monnet and Schuman fits neatly into the neo-functionalist theory of regional integration ... in the context of post-war European integration' (Linter and Mazey, 1991, p. 7). However, the initial basis of agreement was both intergovernmental and neo-functional – on the basis of intergovernmental agreements neo-functionalist explanations were conducive as European integration flourished. The EU represents a rational solution to a historical problem – in the face of necessity it is an example of humanity learning from previous experiences/errors.

The European Economic Community

Initially, the main emphasis of the Treaties provided the basis for a common market. However, through functional processes other areas were incorporated into the Treaties. For instance, through amendments and further treaties the original Article 2 evolved into the following:

> [the] community shall have as its task ... by establishing a common market and an economic and monetary union and by implementing the common policies or activities referred to in Articles 3 and 3a to promote throughout the Community a harmonious development of economic activities, a high level of employment and social protection, equality among men and women, sustainable and non-inflationary growth, a high degree of competitiveness and convergence of economic performance, a high level of protection and improvement of the quality of the environment, the raising of the standard of living and quality of life, and economic and social cohesion and solidarity among Member States. (Foster, 1999, p. 2)

As one can see this identifies functional areas and goes much further than the construction of a common market. There is an evolution to the EU process, which exemplifies interactions between uploading, downloading, crossloading and European integration.

Fundamentally the logic ran that if a single market could work in coal and steel then it could work for all products. Hence, as noted, in 1957 the Treaty of Paris (ECSC), Euratom and the EEC were brought together under the Treaties of Rome. Following the signing of the Treaties there was a feeling of optimism amongst pro-Europeans after the failures of the EPC and EDC. However, this confidence was short lived as the 1960s brought about fracture and disenchantment with the European project. In Article 7 of the Treaty of Paris the institutions of the new community were outlined however during the 1960s when the supranational institutions were put to the test it was the intergovernmental superiority of France that ensured control remained with national parliaments. Under the leadership of de Gaulle argument and rift brought about the French 'empty chair' policy, which saw the European project stall. A clash between de Gaulle's and Monnet's perceptions of the future of Europe was inevitable. The former saw the member state as the primary unit in the EU whereas the latter saw Europe as a whole as the driving force. Monnet envisaged a United States of Europe, de Gaulle a Europe of nation-states; the difference is subtle but very important. One might see Monnet's perspective as neo-functional and de Gaulle's intergovernmental. Indeed, the EEC was faced with precisely the dispute that led to the United Kingdom rejecting membership of the ECSC and the failures of the EDC and EPC. This indicated the re-emergence of intergovernmental variables and the demise of the neo-functional – a reversion to a realist perspective in place of a functional.

The catalyst for conflict between these theoretical perspectives concerned the Common Agricultural Policy (CAP). The European Commission announced that an increase in farm subsidies would be linked to the payment of import levies direct to the Community and extensions to the budgetary powers of the European Parliament (the Assembly). The effects of this constituted a strengthening of a neo-functional or supranational notion of European integration and the intergovernmental element or member state position weakened. In other words, the European Commission and Parliament would have been strengthened to the detriment of the Council of Ministers. In opposition to most member states, France disagreed with these changes so the European Commission pushed for a majority vote in the Council of Ministers. The French representation knew they would lose the vote so failed to attend the meeting and pursued the so-called 'empty chair' policy (not attending meetings) for seven or eight months. It was not until the French forced through the 'Luxembourg Compromise', which shifted policy-making powers back to member states that the project got back on track and even then at a much slower and cautious pace. The Luxembourg Compromise provided 'an arrangement whereby members were permitted to disregard the rules of the Treaty of Rome on majority voting in matters of supreme national concern' (Davies, 1997, p. 1086). At Luxembourg in 1966 de Gaulle forced the Council of Ministers to provide unanimity on cases of important national interest. The issue identified the distinction between intergovernmental and neo-functional perspectives regarding the future of the EU. The French were unhappy with interference from the EU and reacted against the transferral of policy-making sovereignty away from the member state in the direction of the Commission and Parliament. This was going to be an ongoing dispute throughout the EU project with different member states pursuing self-interest and exacerbating the drive towards a single market. This was to become more pronounced as the membership expanded.

With the extension of EU membership to 12 'the point appeared to have been reached at which the European Community was changing itself into a new voluntary association of equal nations – rich and poor. The main criteria for entry, apart from being European was that applicants should have shed the nationalist, imperialistic, and totalitarian traditions of the past' (Davies, 1997, pp. 1086–7). Each had to be recognized in an objective and subjective way by self and other member states as democratic liberal states if membership was to be successful. To be part of the EU member states needed their own civil constitutions to fit with the wider civil constitution under construction through European integration and Europeanization.

Conversely, although membership to the Community was extended in 1973, during the 1970s the EU faced stagnant economic growth. When the European Commission analysed the competitive position of the EU in relation to the United States and Japan it became apparent that problems relating to policy-making had created an uncommon market and the EEC was no more than a glorified Customs Union. Tariff barriers had been removed but Non-Tariff Barriers (NTBs) had obstructed the creation of a SEM. During the 1980s there was a change of emphasis regarding the EU and following White Papers (1984 and 1986), the Cecchini Report (1988) and the Single European Act (SEA) the European project was rejuvenated. Fundamentally, the growing membership activated the extension of the veto but also made clear that if a common market were to be realized then reforms would need to deal with the outmoded or defunct policy-making process. Member states recognized that difficulties with the common market were affecting domestic efficiency. They pressed the EU institutions to deal with these problems and through macro uploading identified how these problems may be rectified. Indeed macro uploading and European integration processes developed means by which NTBs could be dealt with. This involved further integration and the intensification of Europeanization in terms of En1, En2 and En3.

Conclusion

This chapter has outlined the early history of the EU and identified how theoretical perspectives informed its evolution. In the early days the pro-integrationists perceived functionalist and neo-functionalist European Communities that involved taking control of foreign and defence policy. When this was not realized, individuals like Monnet and Schuman had to rethink their strategies and targeted economic domains, which through functional processes could lead towards political integration. Consequently, the success of ECSC was the basis of the EEC and extended membership. However, member states did not simply relinquish sovereignty in areas as easily as Monnet and Schuman had envisaged and in 1966 through the 'empty chair policy', France re-asserted an intergovernmental perspective.

The Luxembourg Compromise allowed both neo-functional and intergovernmental perspectives to be used when explaining European integration but both were flawed when attempting prediction and/or providing explicit links between cause and effect. Both of course failed. Indeed, when we come to the next phase of European integration both theories re-emerge as explanations of the EU and its ongoing development in the form of multilevel governance, state-centricism and Europeanization. A new phase of European integration provided meso theories or frameworks to explain developments and issues. The next chapter highlights these issues in relation to the emerging theoretical perspectives.

5
Macro Uploading and Shared Beliefs: The Single European Act and Economic and Monetary Union

Introduction

In the previous chapter we discussed changes regarding European policy-making and structures following the Second World War. The rationale for European integration was discussed in relation to the theoretical perspectives in terms of neo-functionalism, intergovernmentalism and Europeanization. The paradoxical nature of the ECSC and European Economic Community (EEC) were identified and the dichotomies for member states in terms of their sovereignty in relation to these institutions were analysed. Indeed the previous chapter provided an overview of events of the 1950s and 1960s in relation to theoretical frameworks. This chapter deals with discussions regarding the Single European Market (SEM) and Economic and Monetary Union (EMU) from the early 1970s to the present day (2004).

Each new treaty provided European Union (EU) institutions with some of the authority closely associated with domestic governments. European institutions have played a central role in creating a new impetus towards European integration. In 1984 the European Parliament submitted a draft treaty outlining the establishment of a SEM, followed a year later by the Cockfield White Paper laying out plans for creating a genuine barrier-free internal market by the end of 1992. In 1986 macro uploading became apparent when an intergovernmental conference was convened to negotiate the Single European Act (SEA). These steps deeply influenced Community processes and transformed what was universally viewed as an ineffectual entity into a dynamic force in European and world affairs. Furthermore, in the context of European integration and Europeanization a single currency would have impacts on both members and non-members of the Eurozone. For instance one currency will enable investment and pricing transparency throughout the EU. In terms of financial services the emergence of a single European capital market will allow access to a huge pool of savings. This will enhance cross-border investment and trade should grow. Furthermore, multinationals freed from the financial constraints of national stock markets will become increasingly apparent. Fundamentally, it is argued by Europhiles that the European economy will become more efficient by removing exchange rate uncertainties and transaction costs and allowing pricing transparency in the Eurozone.

This chapter builds on the issues discussed in previous chapters and investigates changes relating to the SEA, Maastricht, Amsterdam and EMU. In each treaty area we observe an interaction between the economic and political domain and the tensions between supranational institutions and member state sovereignty, between neo-functionalism and intergovernmentalism. Finally, during these discussions the text manages to identify and point out instances of Europeanization in terms of En1, En2, En3 and 'content'.

The Single European Act

The SEA was the outcome of macro En2 and European integration and added impetus to the formation of an SEM in that, supranational institutions and member states recognized they needed to deal with Non-tariff Barriers (NTBs) in terms of different rules, regulation and administration costs and so on. The SEA indicated that through harmonization 'the Common Market shall be progressively established during a transitional period of 12 years…divided into 3 stages of 4 year' (HMSO, 1988, Art. 8a). And, 'adopt measures with the aim of progressively establishing the internal market…on 31st December 1992' (ibid., Art. 8b). The existing Common Market was a customs union. NTBs were ensuring that a real common market could not develop. Following calls for action from member states in 1985, the European Commission forwarded plans to remove physical, technical and fiscal barriers between domestic markets by 1992. Indeed, the EU had to face wide-scale re-regulation, which in some areas constituted deregulation. The SEA was a political mechanism for overcoming barriers to trade. It builds on existing policy and extended the powers of the European Parliament. However, the two main objectives incorporated 'co-operation procedure' including Qualified Majority Voting (QMV) and a road map for 1992 and the ongoing programme. These two issues were extremely important because on the one hand harmonization of legislation was necessary to create an SEM and on the other if this legislation was to be implemented, policy-making procedures needed reform. Effectively, we can observe macro En2 and European integration dealing with the deficiencies of the common market. The process is interactive and vacillates between neo-functional and intergovernmental variables and illustrates the different levels of governance.

The SEA outlined the pursuit of an SEM in goods, services, capital and labour and QMV as the means of achieving this market. Through QMV, legislation that had been accumulating for more than 20 years could be dealt with and a common market, or SEM, realized. However, not all policy domains were covered by QMV for instance, member state governments can still veto issues such as taxation. These areas are seen as issues of importance to member states and identify what member state governments perceive as the line between supranational and intergovernmental domains. Overall, although an SEM or common market had been pursued since 1987, with the harmonization of a number of sectors and the realization of cross-border trade, some member states perceived the most encroaching NTB as separate currencies; an issue that would be dealt with by the Maastricht Treaty.

Through the pursuit of the SEM, the EU organized a structured system of legal rules with its own sources, and its own institutions and procedures for making, interpreting and enforcing those rules. The EU treaties have incrementally created an evolutionary legal system which, on the entry into force of each treaty, became an integral part of the legal system of the member states. At the Hague Conference in May 1948, it was held that the time had come for the nations of Europe to transfer certain sovereign rights in order to exercise those rights jointly. 'The states have thus conferred on the Community institutions powers to take measures ... thus submitting their sovereign rights to a corresponding limitation' (Case 17/67 *Newman v Hauptzollant Hof* [1967] ECR 441, 453).

The two main mechanisms that create legislation are regulations and directives. The treaties define a regulation as that which will have 'general application. It shall be binding in its entirety and directly applicable in all member states' (HMSO, 1988, Art. 189). This was emphasized in a 1970s judgment where it was held that a regulation 'renders automatically inapplicable ... any conflicting provisions of current national law – in so far as they ... take precedence ... in the territory of each member state' (Case 106/77 *Amministrazione delle Finanze dello Stato v Simmenthal SpA* [1978] ECR 629, 643). Indeed, it is clear, that national law is subordinate to the wording of a regulation. However, in respect of directives the Treaty provides that they shall 'be binding, as to the result to be achieved upon each member state to which it is directed, but shall leave to the national authorities the choice of form and method' (HMSO, 1988, Art. 187 (3)). The main difference is that a regulation is automatically downloaded in its entirety while a directive must be transposed into national law within the prescribed implementation period. Both regulations and directives involve macro, micro uploading and European integration when they are being developed. However, directives provide the opportunity for diversity in downloading; elements of which can be crossloaded once member states have individually interpreted EU policy mechanisms.

Spillover, financial services and European integration

As noted, Cecchini (1988) forwarded an argument for the provision of an SEM. The report illustrated the economic rationale for the SEA (1987) that needed to be taken on board, if the impasse that the European project had been experiencing was to be overcome. If a common market were to be realized then further European integration would be necessary. Cecchini (1988) proposed that national standards and regulations were what European businesses perceived as the second most important NTB to be removed. The importance of the service sector was not underestimated in the report, although the extent to which the figures may now be relied upon are debatable. This chapter does not wish to give a prognosis on the validity of Cecchini's calculations. It does, however, wish to draw on certain qualitative conclusions that the report displayed. Member states were prepared to give up certain controls in the financial services sector so as to take advantage of a larger market place. This of course was beneficial for both domestic and EU environments and illustrated elements of neo-functionalism, intergovernmentalism and Europeanization.

Cecchini (1988) argued that the role of the service sector in Europe was one of

> growing importance [and that] the potential for much more significant growth is being artificially pinned back by regulations which significantly inhibit the free flow of services and thus the free play of competition between companies. (ibid., p. 37)

Cecchini spoke of the pivotal role that financial services would have in the creation of the single market.

> Basing its figures on a survey conducted on the three main areas of financial services activity...the report forecasts gains of ECU 22,000 million for the eight Community countries Belgium, France, Germany, Italy, Luxembourg, Netherlands, Spain and the UK ... the value-added generated by the credit and insurance sectors alone accounted for some 6.5% of the Community's gross domestic product in 1985...The benefits would be even greater if the freedom to provide within a European financial common market could be linked immediately to a common currency, since exchange costs would disappear and businesses and individual consumers could achieve substantial savings. (European Document, 4/1989, p. 7)

In addition, the freedom to provide cross-border financial services as well as liberalized capital movements would create a more attractive environment for financial business and an efficient means of channelling savings into investment projects.

> The difficulties created by national capital markets in the EU were highlighted in a Commission report dated April 1983. The Commission report identified that gross savings in the EU amounted to ECU 430,000 million and in the USA,

ECU 340,000 million. However, the amount mobilised for investment in the EU's five leading markets (France, Germany, Italy, the Netherlands and the UK) was less than in the USA (ECU 212,000 million in the USA, ECU 142,000 million in the EU). This illustrated the difficulty of mobilising capital in smaller national financial markets. (ibid.)

Financial services such as banking and insurance will be among those to benefit most from the removal of all barriers and the completion of a large internal market. (cited in European Document, 4/1989, p. 18)

The SEA necessitated a number of amendments concerning the free movement of services and capital that are displayed in Articles 43–60 of the consolidated version of the Treaty (Foster, 1999). These illustrate institutional and cultivated spillover and are the basis from which further functional spillover could take place. Macro En2 and European integration formulated the SEA, elements of which were downloaded to individual member states. The SEA then provided the basis for micro En2 further European integration, En1 and En3.

The SEM programme incorporated a continuous process of change that built on the basic tenets of the Treaties of Rome (1988, Arts 2 and 3) and is one that has evolved as further treaties have come into effect. This process of change had already begun and has carried on in a post-SEM Europe. In terms of financial services a number of directives and regulations have been developed in terms of micro uploading and downloaded to the domestic domain. These legislative mechanisms have aided the development of the SEM and provided the basis for the next stage of integration or the completion of the single market through implementation of monetary union. This was to be achieved through the Maastricht Treaty.

The Maastricht Treaty: economic and political integration

The Maastricht Treaty deals with a number of issues that include: subsidiarity, a single economy and currency, European citizenship, the social charter and an extension of the EU's policy-making capabilities through the co-decision procedure. Each of these areas enhanced certain aspects of neo-functional and intergovernmental understandings of the EU. For example, for some subsidiarity indicated a multilevel governance perspective of European policy-making while for others it clearly identified that decisions should be taken at the domestic rather than EU level, that it was effectively state-centric. When Jacques Delors was asked what subsidiarity meant, he answered that it was a 'state of mind'. It can either mean more policy-making for the EU domain, the member states or even the regions. Article 3b of Maastricht and Article 5 of the Consolidated Treaties point out that the EU will

> act within the limits of the powers conferred by this treaty and the objectives assigned to it therein. In areas, which do not fall within its exclusive competence, the Community shall take action, in accordance with the principle of subsidiarity, and only insofar as the objectives of the proposed action cannot be sufficiently achieved by the Member States and can therefore by reason of the scale or effects of the proposed action, be better achieved by the Community. (see Foster, 1999, p. 4)

For some subsidiarity indicated that decisions should be taken as close to the individual as is possible that is, local decisions should be taken at the local level, regional at the regional, national at the national and European at the European. In this context, street lighting should be dealt with at the local or regional level and environmental policy at the European. However, what about when environmental issues touch the local regional or national level how should instiututions demarcate what decisions should be taken where? This is one of the difficulties with EMU; those in the Eurozone have already transferrd policy-making powers regarding economic policy to the European level. Indeed, economic decisions are taken at the EU level and downloaded through member state and regional institutions. The single economy was an extension of the pursuit of the SEM and EMU was an important part of this process.

Implementing the euro

Article 106 of the original Treaty of Rome (HMSO, 1988) identified a monetary committee to review the monetary and financial situation of member states and the European Community and report its findings and opinions to the European Commission and Council of Ministers. Indeed, Article 106 was the embryo of EMU and by 1997 the Consolidated Treaties outlined the transfer to monetary union in Articles 98–124 (Foster, 1999, pp. 26–38). The United Kingdom was not a member at the outset of the EU and therefore had little impact in the formulation of the initial treaty and even though it was involved in the negotiations on the Maastricht Treaty John Major negotiated an opt-out from EMU in 1991, the same opt-out exercised by Tony Blair when the currency was launched in 1999. The original treaties carried with them tacit agreement for closer economic and monetary union – which is an example of Monnet's functional philosophy of developing political and economic integration.

Debates relating to a single currency were rife throughout the 1960s and by the early 1970s two main theoretical perspectives had emerged. These different perspectives were labelled the monetarist and the economist schools. The monetarist school argued for immediately fixed exchange rates while the economists wanted market co-ordination and harmonization prior to fixed exchange rates. These were attempts at macro uploading and in 1970 the Council of Ministers set up a group, led by Pierre Werner, to study these rival proposals.

The Werner group represented an interaction between macro En2 and European integration which led to an attempted compromise between the two schools and argued that member states should pool their reserves and settle their deficits and surpluses through EEC financial arrangements. The Werner group further recommended that member states should agree exchange rate parities and these should be adjusted less and less frequently until 1980 when they should be irrevocably fixed and eventually, replace member state currencies with a single currency.

Of course, because of intergovernmental variables, limitations regarding recognition and shared beliefs this timetable failed to materialize. However another attempt at the realization of a single currency was launched in 1979 through the European Monetary System (EMS). The nine members participated and all but one joined the Exchange Rate Mechanism (ERM). Members of the ERM agreed parity values for each national currency, which could only be changed through consensus. The ERM agreement prescribed that rates should be kept within 2.25 per cent (exceptionally 6 per cent) either side of the agreed parity. For instance, if the lira fell 2.5 per cent against the franc then both Italy and France should buy lira with francs. However, the weak currency partner would have usually taken action before the parity threshold was reached. Action may have taken the form of supporting the lira by selling another currency, for example, dollars, raising interest rates or increasing tax rates and reducing government expenditure. It was uncertain how far tightening fiscal policy would affect the exchange rate in an environment of no capital controls. Of course there was always the possibility of devaluation. Once again an interaction between macro En2 and European integration had taken place, but on this occasion downloading was successful and the basis of EMU was formulated.

Throughout the 1970s and the 1980s the type of monetary union that the EU should have and the means by which it should be achieved was debated in some detail. Each member state developing its preferences and through macro uploading pressing for these at the EU level. The main types of monetary union that were discussed were a currency union, an exchange rate union and a parallel currency. A currency union required perfect mobility of capital, a fully integrated financial sector and one supplier of currency; European Central Bank (ECB). An exchange rate union allowed greater autonomy for member states in that the national central banks remain in control of currency supply and exchange rates. Finally, a parallel currency was where the euro would have competed with other member state currencies. This was the type of monetary union supported by John Major's government and was the form that it attempted to upload into the final decision. However, most member states saw the advantages of a currency union, which they thought would eliminate exchange rate uncertainty and stimulate business and competition. Furthermore, it was thought that trade and investment growth rates would increase and currency and interest manipulation for political purposes would be overcome. The disadvantages would involve the loss of monetary and exchange rate policies to enable domestic objectives and the power to devalue to offset inflation.

Through uploading and European integration the Delors Plan finally brought elements of a currency and exchange rate union into a workable strategy for designing EMU. This was outlined in three stages in the Treaty of Maastricht (1992). Stage three came into operation in 1999 when intra-exchange rates were fixed and after three years (January 2002) the euro appeared. Indeed, in July 2002 member state currencies ceased to exist. In addition, in 1999 the ECB assumed control of the currency union's monetary and exchange rate policies to ensure price and currency stability. 'Despite British scepticism, the majority of EU states pressed ahead both with EMU and the euro. This sharpened the debate within Britain' (Gamble and Kelly, 2002, p. 97). In other words member states and EU institutions were committed to economic and monetary integration and involved themselves in protracted periods of uploading, downloading, cross-loading and European integration processes.

The opt-out experience: downloading in the absence of uploading?

The United Kingdom attempted to involve itself in macro uploading but since it used its opt-out in 1999 its influence in fiscal and monetary matters has been limited. One of the main reasons the United Kingdom did not join in 1999 was because it was further advanced in its economic cycle than the rest of the EU. However, one reason why the members of the euro have successfully aligned their economies is because they said they would and the markets believed they would. The spectacular convergence of interest rates was testimony to this. Through the publication of the five economic tests the United Kingdom has given a signal that it wishes to join the euro and just like Italy's or Portugal's, UK interest rates are converging with Eurozone interest rate (at the time of writing the United Kingdom 3.75 per cent, the Eurozone 2.0 per cent). UK policy has been designed to ensure that as interest rates align and that convergence continues rather than dissipates. The Treasury considered that we needed a 'clear and unambiguous' proof of the economic benefits the euro has to offer and set out five economic tests, which must be met before membership is considered. These are:

(i) Evidence that the United Kingdom has achieved sustainable convergence with the Eurozone economy.
(ii) Indications of flexibility in the UK economy that it can adapt to unexpected economic events.
(iii) Assurance that there will be good conditions for business to make long-term decisions regarding investment in the United Kingdom.

(iv) The effects on UK financial services.

(v) The effects on UK employment.

Government admitted that the tasks are challenging and believed that deciding to join during this Parliament (2001–present) is not impossible but extremely difficult. However, preparations for a debate and referendum have already begun.

Kingsdown (1995) outlined the persistent wait and see attitude of most UK sectors when the UK business community considered that if there was EMU and if it worked, it would be in the United Kingdom's interest to be part of it. Second, that EMU incorporated immense complexities and uncertainties. Third, that the system could be flawed because it may be launched without sufficient economic convergence between the member states and that there was not enough political accountability built into the system. Furthermore, the system did not provide fiscal flexibility to offset the loss of national exchange rate and monetary flexibility. Indeed, because of the stance taken by the United Kingdom on the issue of EMU its ability to participate in macro uploading has been limited.

Many of the issues outlined by Kingsdown (1995) have been incorporated in the United Kingdom's five tests and in some instances it has become apparent that one interest rate is not comfortable for all participating member states. The interest rate is an explicit form of downloading as is the activation of the Stability and Growth Pact (SAGP) which requires that 'national governments adhere to limitations on national deficit and debt levels' (McKay, 2002, p. 79). However, we have recently witnessed member states such as Germany, France and Portugal indicating the constraining aspects of the SAGP in times of low growth/recession who argued for some flexibility, so as to stimulate growth. This identified an example of macro uploading and a re-assessment through European integration procedures of fiscal policies. Indeed, there is some discussion regarding the UK model which considers that deficits and debt should be assessed over the economic cycle, rather than being rigidly adhered to at all times. This could be seen as uploading from the UK government even though it is not a member of EMU, or it may be considered as a form of VPT/En3.

Furthermore, we should not forget that a number of member states are politically committed to EMU. Are we to believe that they have spent years on a senseless adventure that is bound to fail? Considering the economic management of some of these member states, will they not correct defects in EMU with regard to their experiences? No doubt they would, which would intensify uploading by member states and increase European integration through supranational institutions.

HM Treasury (1999) identified key stages for changeover to the euro. In the next UK Parliament a decision to join would be followed four months later by a referendum. If the referendum was positive that is, the UK people decide to join, membership of the euro would take place over the next 24–30 months. Euro cash would appear following a period of fixed exchange rates and sterling would disappear six months later. The changeover would take no longer than 40 months. However, the second term of office, or the Parliament to which the document alluded, is nearly completed and it is now likely that this process will take place in an expected third term. The changeover plan does not give a precise time-scale for membership following a 'yes' vote in the referendum because a number of imponderables need to be dealt with. There is uncertainty regarding the state of readiness of the banks and revenue departments in terms of their ability to deal with the euro.

Prior to membership EU institutions would assess UK performance against certain criteria. 'Before the UK could join the European Commission and the European Central Bank (ECB) would report to the Council on whether the UK had achieved a high degree of sustainable convergence' (HM Treasury, 1999, p. 4). Some of the tests set out by the Treasury adhere to certain EU stipulations. However, European institutions may respond to the United Kingdom's commitment to join by aiming to make life easier rather than more difficult for the United Kingdom. They could do this by not excluding the United Kingdom from key decisions relating to the euro or provide avenues for macro uploading and soften European integration procedures by being flexible when it comes to membership of Exchange Rate Mechanism Two (ERM2). In or out of the single currency the euro will define the United Kingdom's position in the EU and the world for many years to come. The United Kingdom may stay out of the euro but it will be difficult to keep the euro out of the United Kingdom. As noted above, the euro is already impacting on UK financial services regulation. Europeanization of the UK economy is already underway even though it has opted out. Downloading takes place even though in some areas ability to upload has been minimized.

The euro will continue to have a significant affect on UK business. Companies will be able to account, issue shares and pay taxes in euros. The Eurozone is our largest trading partner and accounts for 55 per cent of overseas trade. In this context, impacts on business will take three forms. First, businesses will need to get used to being paid in euros and shouldering the exchange rate risk this involves. This will also be true for pricing strategies when pursuing new business. Second, UK companies are unlikely to be immune from the increased price harmonization that price transparency is likely to engender. Finally, the Bank of England will need to set interest rates higher than the euro rate to achieve a stable pound–euro exchange rate, while at the same time seeking convergence. Furthermore, it is likely that consumers will benefit from cheaper goods. Retailers will no longer be able to hide behind exchange rate fluctuations. The euro will make it easier to compare prices and differences should level out. Cross-border shopping will be possible in the Eurozone and it will be easier for wholesalers to obtain better deals, the benefits of which should be passed on to the consumer.

A large number of companies in opt-out and accession states will carry out their internal accounting in euros. For instance Eurozone based companies have informed suppliers in states external to the Eurozone that they would like goods priced in euros. This means that UK companies undertake transactions with other UK companies in euros. Furthermore, it is likely that the increasing number of Pan-European companies will insist on using the euro as their operating currency. UK Small and Medium Size Enterprises (SMEs) will be caught up in the supply chain and will need to bill larger companies in euros. Each of these factors point to the likelihood of the euro becoming a prime business currency in opt-out and accession states. Mortgages may be taken out in euros. Obviously most borrowers would rather pay their mortgage in the same currency as they are paid as exchange rate fluctuations may undermine the benefits of a euro mortgage. However, as some companies are considering paying their employees in euros and as the euro interest rate is lower than the United Kingdom's some individuals may find the proposition attractive. In this context, there is a mixture of En1 and En3 through vertical policy transfer with EU companies forcing UK companies into dealing with the euro and Eurozone economic and monetary policy.

Eurocreep and the loss of sovereignty in terms of monetary policy that is, setting interest rates and being unable to alter exchange rates against other currencies are intergovernmental objections to the euro. Regarding this objection it has been argued that in many cases monetary policy is determined by external influences. However, this does not deal with the difficulties relating to the one-size fits all interest rate where uploading is minimized and downloading maximized. Furthermore, we can identify problems with the SAGP in that even though tight guidelines have been downloaded in some instances these have been disregarded and illustrate elements of diversity. What is evident is that the SAGP is unworkable and member states are already crossloading and uploading preferences regarding change.

One may argue that the longer member states remain out of the Eurozone, in the face of ongoing Europeanization, the greater the disadvantages become. Indeed, the more difficult it may prove to gain entry. External to the Eurozone member state currencies could become very unstable. Eurozone economies of scale could increasingly dwarf any advantages that the opt-out states enjoy. Furthermore, with respect to all opt-out but with particular attention to the United Kingdom the level of direct inward investment may change if they/it remain outside of the Eurozone. In 2003 Nissan indicated a broader impact of Europeanization in that UK membership of the euro would have a significant impact on decisions regarding future investment. At a speech to Japanese business leaders in Tokyo, Tony Blair made it clear that despite Treasury fears 'over the long term, monetary union is in the national interest' GDP would increase by 0.25 per cent per year over 30 years this would mean an increase of between 5 and 9 per cent. As Tony Blair noted 'enough money … to pay for the whole National Health Service' (Observer, 2003, p. 11). In this way, Europeanization through downloaded convergence criteria (En1) and structural reforms (En3), such as changes to the UK housing market, would eventually provide the basis of Eurozone membership. However, an important factor was that they would only need to be started rather than completed and if the United Kingdom was 'on its way to convergence with other European economies (this) would markedly shorten the timescale of joining the single currency' (ibid.).

A primary concern for the United Kingdom was the curtailment of macro uploading in EU economic and political matters. There was an erosion of the United Kingdom's political influence in terms of European economic decision-making, for example, European interest rates would be set without UK input. The euro impacts on a number of issues relating to business and finance and membership would allow UK uploading in these very important areas. Of course, in respect of legislation regarding financial services the United Kingdom is in a position to upload preferences. However, in terms of decisions relating to interest rate and fiscal policies at present it cannot. Indeed, the euro is part of the completion of the SEM and as long as the opt-out and accession states are external to the Eurozone they negate influence in the ongoing development of the SEM and EU project.

Even though EMU has gone ahead further compromise will need to be made and 'despite all precautions, monetary union will still be something of a leap in the dark. There is no precedent for such a move to a single currency … Even if the rules have been well prepared and the institutions properly designed, there can be no certainty in advance that it will work perfectly in practice' (Kingsdown, 1995, p. 5). However, Eurozone states have invested time and money in the project and are committed to its success. At the moment we may simply wish for economic integration. However, is it possible to stop at EMU? Is EMU an incremental step to closer political ties and ultimately political union? Overall, EMU is a means by which recognition can be realized and is an intensification of the European civil constitution. The EU project has been taken forward in areas such as common foreign and security policy, European citizenship, social charter and the co-decision procedure which were introduced in the Treaty of Maastricht but then given in more detail in the Treaty of Amsterdam.

The Treaty of Amsterdam

The Treaty of Amsterdam argued that the EU needed to be more accountable and relevant to ordinary people. Maastricht mentioned areas such as citizenship but had really concentrated on EMU. With this in mind Amsterdam concentrated on issues that would bring the EU and its citizens closer. The areas it specifically deals with are as follows:

Unemployment: (a) co-ordinating strategies, (b) financing pilot projects.

Social needs: (a) combating discrimination, poverty and social exclusion, (b) eliminating inequality, (c) enhancing consumer protection, (d) extending human rights, (e) providing further freedom, security and justice.

Enhancing effectiveness on the international stage in terms of: (a) common strategies, (b) constructive absenteeism.

Preparations for enlargement in terms of: (a) a more democratic Europe, (b) reforming institutions to make them more effective, (c) furthering decision-making powers for the EU, (d) reinforcing subsidiarity, (e) upholding the principle of democracy and accountability.

Member states needed to respond to global problems as a unit. Each of these areas were uploaded by member states and processed through European integration procedures and many are now being downloaded to member states, for example, Working Time Directive.

The Treaty of Amsterdam also incorporated the Schengen Agreement (the removal of internal frontier checks) and enhanced co-operation between police forces and legal systems. Moreover, '[a] large part of co-operation in the areas of justice and home affairs [will be] subject to Community rules: the participation of all institutions, the legal review of the European Court of Justice and the use of effective legal instruments' (EUR OP, 1997). The Treaty was signed in October 1997 and came into force following ratification by the UK Parliament. The Treaty of Nice took up many of these issues and reinforced changes relating to policy-making and Enlargement. Each of the treaties provided the basis for change in EU policy-making procedures and identified areas for further European integration and Europeanization. Once in motion national and sub-national actors became involved in the development of legislation and the process of macro and micro uploading.

Conclusions

Each treaty and EU/domestic reform has been developed through En2, En1 European integration and En3; through intergovernmental and neo-functional variables in the form of multilevel governance. The decision to add impetus to European integration through the SEA, QMV and Maastricht Treaty negotiations indicated political will in terms of uploading and downloading. For instance, even though the United Kingdom had not joined the Eurozone the euro was still impacting on UK policy-making and economic decision-making. Opt-out states were part of the EU and SEM and adhered to rules and regulations formed through this membership. Indeed, in areas where EMU and SEM interacted, as with accession states, they were forced to deal with euro-based impacts.

In wholesale markets in particular and financial services in general the 'euro has spurred a quantum leap' in the integration of EU financial markets (European Commission, 1999b). Mario Monti, the then European Commissioner for Financial Services informed the Financial Services Policy Group (FSPG) in 1999 that, 'the single market for financial services is crucial to the success of the euro and Economic and Monetary Union. We need to work together co-operatively and with an open mind to forge agreement on a series of incremental pragmatic steps to facilitate cross-border provision of services while ensuring confidence on the part of users' (European Commission, 1999, p. 1). The FSPG was set up to discuss these issues and participate in the formulation of the Financial Services Action Plan (FSAP). In other words, the euro had lent an impetus to the uploading procedures from member states and intensified European integration through European Commission moves to outline the debate and indicate necessary changes for a single market in financial services. Furthermore, as the European Commissioner for Competition Policy Mario Monti pointed out over the last ten years 'the opening of new possibilities and the introduction of the euro have probably been the two major external factors affecting the evolution of the security industry in the EU' (European Commission, 2002, p. 1).

As noted by Gamble and Kelly (2002) 'although Britain remained outside of the euro, it was still part of the EU, a signatory of the treaties, and therefore could not avoid being affected by the broader process of EMU with its separate dimensions of monetary policy, fiscal policy, and employment policy' (p. 98). This chapter identified arguments relating to membership of the SEM and the effects non-membership of the Eurozone may have in terms of macro uploading, downloading and European Integration procedures. Chapter 6 deals with uploading in general and concentrates on micro En2 in the form of sub-national interests.

6
Micro Uploading: Sub-national Interests and Supranational Institutions

Introduction

The two previous chapters in this part have primarily dealt with macro uploading and downloading. This chapter deals with micro uploading in the form of interest group intermediation and other sub-national actors. A number of commentators have provided analyses of the formation and development of sub-national interests at the European level and their interaction with the European policy-making institutions (Grant, 1995; Kirchner, 1980; Lieber, 1974; Mazey and Richardson, 1993, 1996; Sidjanski, 1970). Sidjanski (1970) proposed that interest groupings established themselves at the European level because they recognized a new policy-making centre. As the European Union (EU) began to affect certain interests, organizations congregated around the new institutions 'sometimes ... prompted by invitation or even pressure from the Commission' (p. 402). Mazey and Richardson (1996) identified interest group/European Commission interaction and provided clear evidence that consultation and lobbying are prolific. Furthermore, there have been numerous studies of sector specific sub-national interests and their interactions with EU policy-making institutions (Camerra-Rowe, 1996; Coen, 1997, 1998; Greenwood, 1995, 1997; Greenwood and Cram, 1996; Greenwood et al., 1992; Mazey and Richardson, 1996; McLaughlin, 1995; McLaughlin and Greenwood, 1995; McLaughlin et al., 1993).

This chapter will overview a number of these studies and provide examples of uploading in relation to financial services in general and then concentrate on micro uploading in relation to life insurance. Following this discussion of life insurance the chapter makes generalizations regarding financial services that are discussed in more detail in Part III.

Micro uploading and sub-national interests

Camerra-Rowe (1996) identified that different sectors undertake different strategies when it comes to lobbying European institutions. Firms often have an incentive to lobby (European institutions) directly. 'However, it is rare for a firm, even a large one, to rely on one channel of representation' (p. 6). Coen (1997, 1998) indicated that large companies lobby the European Commission directly. A high degree of lobbying strategies and activities are undertaken by large companies in the EU and that 'this new lobbying activity is a function of the changing regulatory competencies of the European Commission' (Coen, 1998, p. 76). This provided the basis for a number of difficulties. Companies that lobby directly undermine the role of interest groups because the message they carry may not represent the whole sector. Furthermore, they may have limited incentives to accommodate their positions with the collective, because they are able to lobby themselves. They may also force interest groups to reach consensus, which may lead to the acceptance of the lowest common denominator and undermine the effectiveness of the interest group.

Sub-national activity could be identified through large companies lobbying EU institutions directly or through interest group intermediation, which meant there were different ways micro uploading could be undertaken. However, even though 'single firm representation is heard (by the European Commission), the firm concerned, is usually told that the Commission would wish to explore the issue further by talking to the interest group concerned in order to ensure that it gets a more representative opinion' (Greenwood, 1997, p. 4). Furthermore, even though there are a number of interest groups from separate member states, competition gives way to co-operation through resolving issues at the EU level (Browne, 1990). This is achieved by moving the 'analysis from the domain level to the issue level in order to provide a common substantive context for elite/pluralist interpretations' (ibid., p. 477). Coen (1998) also considered that through issue-based politics the European Commission had 'institutionalised its bargaining position with business and created a form of "elite pluralism" ... [which] requires that firms develop ... pan-European political alliances in exchange for access to restricted entry forums' (p. 77). Large companies are forced into involving themselves with interest groups and networks of companies if they are to participate in successful uploading.

Micro uploading: the case of the EU insurance industry

The European insurance industry mainly consists of medium-size enterprises, which lack the political capability and resources to undertake direct action in Brussels (this is gradually changing through mergers and acquisitions). Because of this, both national and European interest groups have greater influence over their membership and the European Commission. Companies need to accept interest groups 'policy position, even if it does not take account of their particular interests, because they cannot effectively represent their own views. As a result, and paradoxically, the more fragmented insurance sector was better able to undertake collective activity in pursuing Community policy' (Camerra-Rowe, 1996, p. 21).

Even though Allianz could lobby directly, it only did so intermittently. However, Allianz was closely linked with the national association and on some issues the company's position became the national association's position. This was verified by Small and Medium Size Enterprises (SMEs) who took care not to contradict Allianz in the formulation of policy (ibid.). In addition, a change in the position of a member state interest group can also have an effect on EU policy. For instance during the early 1990s the French interest group started to change its stance regarding uploaded perspectives and 'gradually swung to join the liberalising elements of the Comité Européen des Assurances (CEA)' (Vipond, 1995, p. 107).

Browne (1990) investigated whether interest groupings existed that integrate policy and issues within a domain. Three generations of life assurance directives indicated an integrated policy in the domain of financial services and the Third Life Assurance Directive as an issue within this policy domain. The Third Life Assurance Directive is a narrow issue and this ensured successful legislation. The CEA is concerned with other issues relating to the policy domain of insurance. However, other interest groups deal with policy domains relating to banking, capital markets and pensions, which belong to the domain of financial services. In this way, narrow issues ensure that successes are more likely and frequent. Browne (1990) also considered that interest groups and other lobbying organizations create coalitions in terms of the goals they pursue. This chapter considers that the CEA is an integrated interest group because it has a policy domain that itself became more integrated as European integration intensified. The CEA has become an interest group with a developed issue identity. This is clear in its role as uploader and verified by its activities in the development of insurance regulation. Other interest groupings deal with other parts of the sector, for example European Banking Association (EBA) in the development of banking legislation (this will be discussed in more detail in Part III).

The insurance sector is considered to have a unified and influential interest group because companies need to accept interest group representation. The European Commission prefers to deal with European-wide interest federations rather than representatives of individual or national organizations (OJ/93C 63/03). 'Both the European Commission and the European Parliament frequently stress that they want to speak to European organisations' (Club De Bruxelles, 1994, p. 96). Micro uploading is more likely to be realized in legislation if it comes through unified groupings.

The Treaties of Rome stated that services and capital needed liberalization and harmonization. The Single European Act (SEA) indicated that the 'liberalisation of ... insurance services connected with the movements of capital shall be effected in step with the progressive liberalisation of capital' (HMSO, 1988, Art. 61(2)). And that the 'movement of capital between Member States shall be freed from all restrictions by the end of the first stage at latest' (ibid., Art. 67(2)). If this was to be the case then a number of areas needed to be taken into consideration regarding Non-tariff Barriers (NTBs). Through its concentration on the life insurance industry this chapter and Chapter 7 indicate the technical barriers in respect of regulations that needed harmonization, if a Single European Market (SEM) in life insurance was to be achieved.

Vipond (1995) outlined a view of insurance representation at the EU level and indicated how national positions are compromised in the main European interest group, the CEA. As noted in Chapter 5, Cecchini (1988) undertook an analysis of the benefits to be gained from the single market and the extent to which insurance was an important aspect of this. A political emphasis is illustrated in the European Commission White Paper (1985), the SEA (1997), the Treaties of Rome (1988), the Maastricht Treaty (1991) and the Commission Report (1992). Randone (1990) and Canzano (1994) indicated that the way forward was in planning and creating a strategy for EU financial services and acknowledged the need for legislation that facilitated cross-border trade. In response to macro uploading the insurance industry identified that a response was necessary in terms of micro uploading not simply from a member state perspective but one from a European perspective. For instance Pool (1992) concluded that 'insurers are certainly much better organised as a pressure group than the other players in the insurance markets. Even they, however, have not always found it easy to arrive at a common perception of what a common market should mean for them' (p. 11).

The CEA was established in 1953 and acted on behalf of its membership regarding European issues for many years. The main objectives of European interest groups are two-fold. First, they should 'promote the exchange of information and try to find common denominators' (Kirchner, 1980, p. 109). Second, 'co-ordinate and exert pressure for adopted policies through the European organisations and the national affiliations on both the EC and the national government' (ibid.). In the context of insurance, the CEA certainly achieved this objective in its role as micro uploader. Pool (1992) illustrated the link between the evolution of the EU, its growing membership, its institutions and the progression of its legal framework. He described how the Commission and the treaties are part of the policy-making process. However, he did not indicate whether or not the insurance industry had a part to play in this process; the CEA contended that it did and that as an interest group, it uploaded information and preferences and were central to the process.

Considering that diverse life insurance legislation existed throughout the EU, how was an SEM in life insurance to be achieved? (Hofstede, 1995). Eltis and Spencer (1993) acknowledged this problem and considered that mutual recognition and the co-ordination of essential minimum levels of supervision and co-operation between supervisors was the way forward. This is an important factor in the development of cross-border trade and an issue investigated further in Part III when shared beliefs formation and downloading a form of 'competent authority' and supervisory regime are discussed in more detail. However, when a number of diverse regulatory structures and supervisory regimes exist how does the financial services sector agree on the most acceptable structure and regime? Indeed to each member state it is very likely that their structure and regime would be most acceptable.

Loheac (1992) argued that the third generation of insurance directives constituted a 'cultural revolution' which affected all European financial sectors and that the operation of financial services would not be left unaffected by legal developments in the EU. All member state sectors would be affected in some way by the changes in legislation and, as integration grew, differing legislative norms would become more apparent and the more difficult it would become to meet minimum conditions to overcome this diversity (Loheac, 1991). Loheac (1992) identified regional grouping through integration and a convergence of regulation, which he hoped would create further trading between member states. In this way, diversity would not be completely prohibited but minimized to the extent that cross-border trade would be possible.

Heseltine (1992) foresaw greater harmonization in the SEM and proposed further consultation with business and welcomed constructive dialogue between the insurance industry and government. He stated that this was 'an absolutely essential foundation' (p. 5) for cross-border trade in financial services as were the close relations between the industry and the Department of Trade and Industry (DTI). Heseltine (1992) further argued a UK position, in the context, of macro and micro uploading; that 'less legislation is the UK way' (ibid.) and that he wished to persuade the rest of the EU that this was the appropriate model. Palliser (1992) considered that the insurance industry had been shaped by legislation and 'that in time the harmonisation of regulatory frameworks should introduce open competition in the life insurance market across the Community' (p. 4).

Following macro En2 in the realization of an SEM, micro En2 in relation to financial services intensified with the realization that regulation differences were the main factors undermining the creation of a single market. With regard to this, the European Commission considered that its main objective was to create co-ordinated supervision throughout the EU. Little change was needed to reinsurance because member state reinsurance regulatory structures were similar. However, at the other end of the scale 'divisions appeared most marked in life insurance' (Pool, 1992, p. 179). Schmidt (1989) considered that the freedom 'to provide services throughout the EC is intended to make it possible to exploit the local advantages of production vis-à-vis the customers of other sectors. In both cases the trade barriers contained in the legal framework conditions should be reduced as far as possible by harmonising laws' (p. 16).

Dickinson (1990) contended that a common market in life insurance means 'both the freedom of insurance companies to supply and the freedom of consumers to buy in any country within the Community' (p. 97). He further argued that one of the main difficulties in creating an SEM in financial services was that member states had different legislative environments and regulatory structures. 'Legislative environments vary significantly across the Community...this variation is due to differing local market and regulatory traditions' (ibid., p. 98).

O'Leary (1988) drew attention to the feelings of many UK insurers and their inability to take the SEM as seriously as their continental counterparts. His hope was that such would not continue to be the case as change is continual in the creation of the SEM and it was crucial that the United Kingdom had input into the formulation of the market. Additionally, insurance contracts caused a problem, as they do today.

> Article 25 contains a marketing rule for insurance products...to the single case of contracts in conflict with legal provisions protecting the general good in the Member State in which the risk is situated. The concept of general good...must be understood in the light of...derogation's to freedom laid down by the EEC Treaty are only allowed where there exists in the area considered, mandatory reasons linked to the general good (consumer protection rule) providing that this interest is not already safeguarded by rules to which the undertaking is subject in the Member State in which it has its head office...and providing that the same result cannot be obtained by less stringent rules. (CEA Working Paper, 1990, p. 2)

In the field of insurance services, the concept of the general good has come to play an important role. First, this is so 'because Community insurance directives only partially regulate cross-border insurance activities, and leave room for member state regulation. Secondly, these insurance directives refer explicitly to the general good in relation to the regulation of insurance activities in general and insurance products in particular' (ibid., p. 152). Fundamentally, it would be necessary to monitor the concept of 'general good' very closely if it was not to become an NTB (this is discussed in more detail in Part III).

The main difficulty facing the parties involved was the creation of a single market in life insurance. In insurance, the existing national markets differed significantly in terms of the nature and amount of regulation. They also differed in the nature and variety of products that were offered. The problem the EU and insurance industry faced was how to reconcile the objective of liberalizing the markets, and offering consumers a wide range of choice, with that of satisfying the authorities in all member states that there is adequate protection for the policy-holder and third parties (Fitchew, 1988). This could be achieved through the successful negotiation of shared beliefs and uploading.

By 1992, the specifics of the generation of insurance directives were generally understood. They removed '*a priori* control of policy and rating conditions and replaces it with a non-systematic *a posteriori* communication system; this means that a long continental tradition of material control is abandoned and the essence of – which is attributed to the authorities of the countries office – no longer focused on the products ... but the undertaking itself, its solvency, its shareholding and its management' (Loheac, 1992, pp. 2–3). This should maximize competition in terms of products and increase innovation. However, there was a problem in terms of the 'general good' where member state supervisory authorities may outlaw a product if it is deemed risky. Obviously, this allows those member states with more prescriptive legislation a modicum of protection which may be seen as a barrier. General good is discussed in more detail in Part III.

In general terms, the directives outlined a compromised framework, which once in place relied on the concept of mutual recognition (given the concept of the general good). Once harmonization had taken place, a form of confrontation would occur and 'this confrontation with regulations should result in the different national rules being brought into line with each other: states which have a tradition of strict control will have to ease their regulatory constraints if they want to avoid penalising their own national undertakings ... In the final analysis, the logical consequence would be that a less strict system of control would, in time, set the European standard' (ibid.). This is when diversity of interpretation is either dealt with through further En2 or En3. That is either through further legislation or policy transfer. Indeed, mutual recognition may be considered a mechanism that enables and even encourages policy transfer.

Of course, this could only occur following an initial period of harmonization or re-regulation. Indeed, the Commission saw the creation of the SEM as being pursued through three fundamental means: minimum harmonization, mutual recognition and home country control. However, the 'principle of mutual recognition as a rule only applies to a list of activities generally annexed to the directives (either adopted or in the process of being so) in the financial services ... The approach by the Community authorities in directives on the financial services is essentially institutional and sectoral. The specific features of each financial services sector means that they will be regulated by a body of formally and materially distinct regulations even though overall these texts are based on the same principles (single license)' (Loheac, 1991, p. 408). Minimum harmonization, mutual recognition and home country control form the basis uploaded shared beliefs, differential downloading (diverse interpretation) and crossloading (En3). Uploading (En2) ensures minimum harmonization, home country control diversity in downloading (En1) and as noted mutual recognition crossloading (En3).

Basically, in each specific sector there needed to be agreement on basic rules and these minimum harmonizations were only possible because 'common interest, mutual confidence and a degree of economic convergence exist between EEC member states' (ibid., p. 409). It is on the agreement of this basic legislation that mutual recognition and cross-border trade in life insurance products rely.

Conclusion

This chapter illustrated how the SEM is evolving and indicated how this may be part of integration processes that are further developing the EU. Treaties gave impetus to European integration and through macro and micro uploading industries, sectors and member states are proactive in the formation of the EU and SEM and this necessitates interaction between Europeanization and European integration through further extensions of the treaties. Included in the extensions of the treaties and development of the SEM and EU is the free movement of financial services.

Overall, the continued liberalization of European financial services should suit EU financial services providers. However, although this may be the case, each member state needed to make changes to its regulatory structure and business practices. It was recognized that it was 'essential to overcome ... differences in legal systems and regulations in individual member states in order to create an integrated European insurance market' (Loheac, 1992, p. 4). Even with interest group intermediation and successful micro uploading this had not been completely achieved in the EU, either in insurance or financial services in general. This is because of differential downloading as well as the 'general good' and will necessitate further changes by those involved in the market place, whether or not they participate in cross-border trade. These further changes are discussed in the context of further uploading and downloading in Part III.

The legal effectiveness of the Third Life Assurance Directive in large part 'depends on the good faith of the member states in transposing them into national law' (Fine, 1997, p. 126). Tax issues still impeded the development of a single market for financial services in the EU. Barriers had only been partially removed 'some member states allow tax deductibility of premium only on insurance contracts bought from domiciled insurers, meaning that non-domiciled insurers cannot compete on a level playing field' (Shapiro, 1997, p. 23). These differentials created difficulties and in some instances opportunities for those trading in the SEM. However, gradually the barriers have been removed and through compromised regulatory structures an SEM is gradually developing. Diversity existed in terms of different interpretations of directives or differential downloading. However, through mutual recognition and En3 and further En2 many obstacles were being overcome.

The SEA, Maastricht, Amsterdam, Nice etc., have paved the way for streamlined policy-making, intensive regulation formulation and the development of the SEM. Through harmonized regulation a level playing field is being created and cross-border trade made possible. With the realization of the euro the opportunities offered by an SEM in financial services and life insurance become more realistic. This provided further evidence of the interaction between European integration and Europeanization. The next stage of the process is now in motion. As noted in the previous chapter, through further macro uploading member states put into operation further European integration in European financial services through the Financial Services Action Plan (FSAP). This encourages further Europeanization through micro uploading and eventual downloading.

'In order to be effective Euro-lobbyists, groups must be able to coordinate their national and EC level strategies, construct alliances with their European counterparts, and monitor changing national and EC policy agendas' (Mazey and Richardson, 1993, p. 191). To be effective micro uploaders (sub-national interests) must on the one hand, pursue national preferences, but on the other be ready to compromise these preferences for the good of the sector in general. However, because of their different cultures and understandings about what would be best for an SEM, how may this be accomplished? How are policy-domains and shared beliefs constructed? How do separate member state industries overcome self-interest and work towards collective interest? One thing is for sure, because of different cultural perspectives downloaded directives will not be interpreted and implemented in exactly the same way. Consequently, differentiation regarding market regulation will exist throughout the EU, which causes problems for cross-border trade. Again these issues will be explored in Part III.

This part has identified elements of European integration processes and Europeanization in the evolution of the EU. Initially political philosophy and grand theory were able to explain the process. However, as the EU became more difficult to explain through grand theory and the philosophical perspectives seemed too abstract, meso theory was introduced. In this study, substantive theory is formulated to provide better explanations and understanding of European integration and those changes apparent in the EU. The next part discusses substantive theory in more detail.

Part III

Europeanization as Situation and Process: Synthesizing Theory and Methodology

This part builds on the previous two and identifies specific examples of uploading (En2), downloading (En1), crossloading (En3) and European integration. Chapter 7 outlines the development of shared beliefs (content) in relation to member state regulatory structures. Regulation is broken down into three broad categories and analysed in relation to domestic regulation and desired change within the domestic structure. To ensure acceptable regulation, member state interest groupings through European Union (EU)-wide groupings involve themselves in the development of directives. In this context, they upload preferences and compromise their positions in relation to other member states. This process is made clear in Chapter 8 where the utilization of subnational interests are discussed in relation to some empirical evidence. In such a way we observe micro En2 as 'situation' and 'process' in that there needs to be interaction with European integration.

In Chapter 9 the interaction between European integration and macro En2 is discussed through the development of the Financial Services Action Plan (FSAP). Again the demarcation between the two areas is sometimes difficult to identify but 'situation' and 'process' can be observed. Finally, Chapter 10 outlines four case studies that attempt to concentrate on En1. However, even though cause and effect is clarified through simplification, clear reliability and verification in certain instances is still problematic. Indeed, when attempting a purely positivist analysis in the social sciences, one will always confront these difficulties. Overall, Part III provides an illustration of mixed methodological approaches and theoretical perspectives.

7
Identifying Difference and Potential Shared Beliefs: Domestic Issues and Financial Services Regulation

Introduction

As noted in Part I the European Union (EU) environment (or political space at the EU level) encompasses European integration; uploading, downloading and crossloading incorporate Europeanization. On the one hand, Europeanization can be seen as the source of change in relation to the EU level in terms of European integration and the development of supranationality. On the other hand, European integration can be seen as the source of change and Europeanization the outcome of change on member state's governmental, legal and regulatory structures. Fundamentally, we have interactions between Europeanization and European integration in the construction and perpetuation of supranational institutions and development of EU and domestic policies and systems. Europeanization incorporates uploading from the member states, which can be undertaken by government, interest groups, sectors or companies. At some point Europeanization becomes European integration (this is difficult to pinpoint because of the continual interaction between the two areas) this is where EU institutions develop legislation, which is eventually downloaded to member states. Indeed, change is indicated through European directives and regulations, which, on the one hand, are directly downloaded by the EU and, on the other, downloaded through domestic legislatures. In the latter case, En1 provides the opportunity for interpretation and diversity throughout the EU and En3 with this differentiation through mutual recognition and policy transfer. Through a study of financial services this study illustrates these intricacies.

Howell (2000) identified that in the early 1990s, different member states employed different regulatory structures and supervisory regimes based on cultural considerations. Through analysis and survey Howell (1999, 2000) broke these differences down into liberal, prescribed and state-controlled regulatory structures and identified which of these regimes the member states utilized in their supervisory structures.

Through comparative analysis this chapter allocated member states a position between 1 and 12 on a Regulation Scale (see Figure, 7.1). A totally liberal structure was indicated by point 1 on the scale and a completely state-controlled structure point 12, a prescribed regime existed between points 5 and 8. As the scale displays, this does not mean that there are no differentiations within each regulatory structure but the codification does allow a means of identifying different

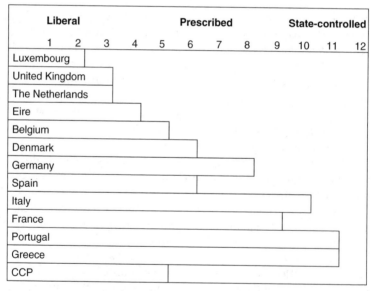

Figure 7.1   Regulation Scale one

Notes: CCP = Compromised Convergence Point (Shared Beliefs); matrix compiled from an analysis of Munich Re (1988); *Financial Times* (1992); *Sigma Re* (1988–93); Pool (1991); BIIC and CEA Working Papers.

Source: Howell (2000).

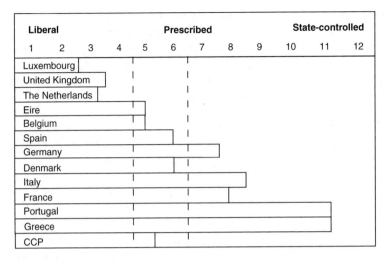

Figure 7.2 Regulation Scale two

Notes: CCP = Compromised Convergence Point; matrix compiled from an analysis of Munich Re (1988); *Financial Times* (1992); Sigma Re (1988–93); Pool (1991); BIIC and CEA Working Papers and survey of insurance.

Source: Howell (1999, 2000).

regulatory structures (see Figures 7.1 and 7.2). Comparative analysis of the regulatory structures of member states illustrate the normative perceptions domestic industries would be aiming to micro upload to the EU, in pursuit of a single market. Each domestic industry had a different cultural tradition in relation to financial institutions and investment. These are illustrated through historical attitudes and economic ideologies, which in turn are exemplified through legislation and the subsequent regulation relating to life insurance (Hofstede, 1995). This chapter provides an overview of these regulatory structures and identifies how differentiated cultural values may be merged into shared beliefs (Garret and Weingast, 1993). The study was undertaken in the early 1990s, so it only deals with the states that were members of the EU during that period.

A liberal regulatory regime

A liberal regulatory regime lies between 1 and 4 on the 12-point Regulation Scale and is characterized by self-regulation with minimal legislation. Four EU life insurance industries were identified as having relatively liberal structures in respect of their regulations. They were the Republic of Ireland (Eire) (point 4), Luxembourg (point 2), the Netherlands (point 3) and the United Kingdom (point 3).

Supervision in all four liberal regulatory structures was based on the concepts of self-regulation for both products and premiums. This is interposed by a regulatory structure of minimal prescription in terms of insolvency regulations and supervisory institutions. For 65 years Dutch regulation was based on 'Wet op Levensverzekering-bedrijf' (WOL), which was established in 1922 following two major insolvencies. This was superseded in 1987 by the 'Wet Toezicht Verzekerings-bedrijf' (WTV), which monitored company insolvency margins through Verzekeringskamer (VK) supervision and started to bring Dutch regulation into line with that illustrated in EU direc-tives. European legislation was downloaded to the Netherlands, which affected the national regulatory structures and consequently impinged on the normative experience of the member state. Such was also clear within the Irish market where most recent legislation attempted to bring it in line with the EU.

The UK industry was initially supervised through the Department of Trade and Industry (DTI) and later by the Treasury and relied on the principle of 'freedom with disclosure'. In general, 'insurers are free to compete as they choose in the marketplace, provided that they meet certain requirements designed to ensure the continuing solvency of all entities underwriting policies of insurance' (*Financial Times*, 1992, p. 291). However, following membership of the EU and a number of company failures, the regulatory framework was inten-sified 'partly through the perceived need to protect policy-holders ... and partly as a result of changes arising from the implementation of European Community directives' (ibid.). In this context there are two rationales for changes to the UK regulatory structure, Europeani-zation through En1 and an internal or domestic rationale.

The Financial Services Act (1986) provided supervision through the Life Assurance and Unit Trusts Regulatory Organisation (LAUTRO) and the Financial Intermediaries Managers and Brokers Association (FIMBRA). However even though these institutions were supposed to be independent, they were closely tied to the financial services sector. This was indicated by the shift towards an institution with greater independence, the Personal Investment Authority (PIA), which was replaced by Financial Services Authority (FSA). The latter institution oversees the whole sector following changes in UK legislation that were linked to both EU directives and domestic difficulties regarding pensions, investment and banking. (The structure of UK regulatory regime and the role of the FSA are discussed in more detail when UK downloading is discussed in more detail later.)

Luxembourg relied on self-regulation and when problems arose, the Officer of the Commissioner for Insurance (OCI) was consulted. However, the OCI could force insurance companies to comply with Article 18 of insurance legislation (24 February 1984) and could ultimately withdraw approval. This 'modified existing legislation in order to bring it into line with existing EU directives' (*Financial Times*, 1992, p. 202) (Co-insurance Directive 78/473 and the First Life Assurance Directive 79/267). Indeed, downloading had already taken place, which identifies the cyclical dimension of the European integration process and the interactions between this and En1, En2 and En3.

Liberal regulatory structures were similar in respect of ideology in that they have an ethos of limited regulation. However, despite these similarities each market has distinct differences. The reason for this lies in diverse interpretations of previous EU directives, which had began to define member state regulatory structures. The differences between the member states in this area do however seem to be diminishing, as European regulation is downloaded into domestic systems. All four liberal member states have brought themselves into line with EU regulation, which means moving towards more rather than less regulation. Each had already begun a process of Europeanization but distinctions still remained. Downloading in financial services had begun in the 1970s and intensified during the 1980s. However, in the 1990s, it was clear that cultural perspectives and interpretations indicated too much diversification which continued to undermine the Single European Market (SEM). This initiated the FSAP, which is discussed in more detail in Chapter 9.

Prescribed regulatory structures

A prescribed regulatory structure may be identified between 5 and 8 on the Regulation Scale and indicated moderate to tight legislation but without or with limited state interference in the companies themselves. Four member states with lesser or greater degrees of prescription were identified: Belgium, point 5 on the scale, Spain and Denmark, point 6, and Germany, point 8.

The Belgian regulatory structure was liberal until 1930 and supervision was limited. However, in the post-war period Belgian legislation and regulation mirrored developments in the EU and through precise downloading its structure evolved in line with EU directives. Belgian regulation was specific in content but allowed general application in respect of product, profitability and the process of contractual obligations in individual cases. Effectively, supervision was non-systematic and allowed for both prudence as well as profitability. Consequently, both company and consumer needs were dealt with through the regulatory structure.

In the 1970s, Belgian regulation was extended and insurance regulated by the Office De Controle des Assurance (OCA), which was monitored by the Ministry for Economic Affairs. Supervision was undertaken through a committee, which interacted with the ministry and indicated necessary changes in regulation and how it should be administered. The committee was made up of six members, who were drawn not only from insurance but the legal profession, other financial institutions and academia. As many areas as possible were involved in regulating insurance in particular and financial services in general. The OCA did not determine policy rates, it simply ensured that legislation was activated and adhered to regarding technical, legal and financial supervision.

The Belgian approach displayed traits of the evolving SEM in financial services and illustrated an attainable compromise between different life insurance regulatory structures. Such an evolution may be found in developing institutions in different member states throughout the EU. Initially, through En2 and shared beliefs, member states realized the necessity of compatible 'competent authorities' or regulators. However, En1 provided the opportunity for interpretation and diversity – whereas in this instance, En3 began to formalize the structures and ensure greater compatibility.

The Spanish regulatory structure was similar to the Belgian, although it did have its own distinct historical and cultural basis. Until implementation of the new Spanish constitution in 1978, insurance was supervised by a legislation ratified in 1912. Indeed, it was not until the (Ley de Ordenación del Seguro Privado, 1984) that there was regulatory provision for solvency, policyholder protection, professional standards and the re-grouping of companies through mergers. Companies in Spain applied to operate in the market, once registered they were monitored regarding solvency, advertising and products and so on by the Dirección General de Seguro, which reported directly to Government.

German insurance and financial services were tightly controlled and companies had to seek approval for product design and policy terms. There were two main items of legislation, which relate to insurance. These were Versicherungsvertragsgesetz (VVG), which regulated the relationship between insurance companies, the insured, policy-holders and beneficiaries; and the Versicherungsaufssichtsgesetz (VAG) which was responsible for regulations relating to the supervisory body Bundesaufsichtsamt fur das Versicherungswesen (BAV). 'The underlying principle of the insurance supervisory law is the system of "substantive state supervision" (materielle Staatsaufsicht)' (*Financial Times*, 1992, p. 103).

BAV set premium rates, specified mortality tables and products, maximum interest rates and expenses. This created a small difference in product prices and led to limited competition regarding product range. Because most companies had a complete product range, competition revolved around bonus distribution. The German structure was highly regulated, which provided expansive consumer protection and safe but low-yielding products. Historically, Germany had undergone two periods of hyper-inflation, which may have much to do with the risk-averse attitude and the factor of limited product innovation. The prevailing legislation and consequent regulatory structure was determined by cultural and socio-historical circumstances.

Denmark was regulated through the Insurance Companies Act (1981), which prescribed public supervision and company format. The Business Competition Act (1989), which supervised monopoly and price control, the Insurance Contracts Act (1930), which concerned relationships between insurance parties; and the Marketing Act (1975) under which the ombudsman assessed whether insurance company marketing activities adhered to accepted practices. In compliance with law 127(3) a division of the Danish Ministry of Finances supervised the industry.

The Danish regulatory structure was prescribed to the extent that Danish companies submitted detailed financial statements, which included annual accounts and group reports. However, in respect of solvency margins, technical reserves and capital adequacy, EU directives provided the regulatory structure. Furthermore, there were more comprehensive directives in respect of non-life insurance, which the Danish have subsequently implemented.

As with the liberal regulatory environments, the prescribed structures illustrate the changes that EU legislation was bringing about with extreme clarity. The lesser-prescribed markets had the fewest changes to make.

Within the prescribed market environments there were differing amounts of prescription. Germany was the most prescribed (point 8 on the scale), whereas in Spain and Denmark (point 6 on the scale) although regulation was tight, more flexibility was allowed. Belgian regulation (point 5 on the scale) indicated most succinctly the impending single market environment in respect of its existing legislation. What was apparent was the consultative nature of Belgian regulatory structure and that this was indicative of EU guidelines. Belgium had been successful in uploading concerns to the EU. Fundamentally, as with the liberal environments through En2 and European integration, a convergence procedure can be detected with regard to EU legislation and consequent domestic regulatory requirements.

State-controlled regulatory environments

State-controlled regulatory structures were identified between points 9 and 12 on the Regulation Scale and four member states were included in this category. These were France (point 9), Italy (point 10), Portugal and Greece (point 11). At the time of the study (1993/94), each had a state-controlled element to their regulatory structures in that there was a preponderance of state ownership.

On the Regulation Scale, state-controlled regulatory structures were categorized in relation to levels of regulation and the percentage of the market controlled by state-owned companies. In France, regulation was extensive. However, 'French insurers used to be seen as ... hidebound by regulatory red tape of the former all powerful Direction des Assurances ... this over simplified view is now dating rapidly' (*Financial Times*, 1992, p. 81). The French insurance industry was supervised by the 'Direction des Assurance', which was instituted by the Ministry of Economy. Rules were strict with regard to individual life insurance business. Approval was needed for product design, premiums and policy conditions. However, changes were underway to alleviate these restrictions. There was also much consultation with regard to regulation changes, and prior to any changes, companies referred to the 'Conseil National des Assurance' (made up of representatives of the insurance industry and authorities).

Greek and Italian financial services were state-controlled, in that state-owned companies existed in the market and enjoyed certain benefits because of this. For instance, 'the Greek market has traditionally been highly regulated ... this situation is in large part a legacy of heavy government control ... [which has] led to administrative rigidity and as a consequence high operating costs' (*Financial Times*, 1992, p. 143). Italian insurance companies were expected to give a percentage of their business to the state controlled Instituto Nazionale delle Assicurazioni (INA). Following 1 April 1987, life companies writing life business for less than 6 years gave 30 per cent of new business, for 6–10 years, 20 per cent and for over 10 years, 10 per cent. This led to unfair competition in the market and allowed the evolution and maintenance of a dominant position (Munich Re, 1988). The Instituto per la Vigilanza sull Assicurazioni Private de Interesse Collectivo (ISVAP) supervised the Italian market. This was set up by the Ministry of Industry and Commerce and gives approval to insurance matters on its findings.

Each member state was highly regulated. However, each member state was becoming less regulated as EU legislation dictated. In Portugal, 51 per cent of the sector remained in state hands and 33 per cent in France (Munich Re, 1988). In all cases, the state-controlled institutions were the largest in the member state financial services sectors and life insurance markets. The Portuguese regulatory structure was supervised by the 'Instituto de Seguros de Portugal' (ISP). Founded in 1982, the ISP initiated the 'Plano da Explarocao' in 1985, which outlined basic standards for life insurance companies. The ISP exercised total control over life insurance companies and required approval for product design, premium rates and policy wording. Furthermore, quarterly returns inclusive of profit projections had to be submitted by all life insurance companies. Indeed this was a market in which companies were open to complete scrutiny.

Regulatory changes in June 1988 allowed greater liberty in Portugal regarding expenses, but the ISP still determined the mortality base and the technical interest rate. However, it was expected that because of extended freedoms with regard to non-life tariffs these would follow in the life insurance market. 'The insurance market is tightly controlled by government regulation. All insurance businesses must be approved by the Portuguese Ministry of Finance', which consulted with the ISP before companies were given approval (*Financial Times*, 1992, p. 232).

Overall, each state-controlled regulatory structure was becoming more liberal (even though some member states needed to be persuaded of this). Through developing shared beliefs, member state financial services sectors recognized that to facilitate competition in the single market they needed to adhere to EU directives, which attempted to harmonize supervision in the direction of liberal/ prescribed structures. In this context, as with other member states, Europeanization was already having an impact on domestic policy prior to the Single European Act (SEA) and intensified following the reforms of the treaties. In each member state, changes were underway to allow greater freedom and enable competitive markets in line with the single market environment. Each of the state-controlled structures had a different cultural tradition and on the Regulation Scale range between 9 and 11 (see Figure 7.1). However, even though each member state within this category was changing its legislation, which would allow greater freedom in the Single European Market (SEM) these different traditions impacted on interpretation and provided the basis for diversity. These issues will be discussed in more detail later when we examine downloading (En1).

Regulatory structures, survey and analysis

The categorization of member state regulatory structures was supplemented by a survey which investigated the perceptions of EU life insurance companies. The purpose of the survey was to gain an understanding of how member state industries viewed their own regulatory structures and what they considered would be most advantageous for them in the developing SEM. Companies were asked to identify, on a scale of 1–12, the level of existing and future domestic and European regulation. The following questions were asked:

(a) How liberal or state controlled is your national life insurance market?

(b) Where would you place the SEM life insurance sector in respect of regulatory freedom?
(c) What type of regulatory environment do you consider that the SEM should be to allow your company its greatest advantage?
(d) What type of regulatory environment do you consider the SEM in life insurance should be to allow the greatest consumer protection?
(e) What type of regulatory environment do you consider the SEM in life insurance should be to allow the greatest consumer choice?

The survey was distributed between November 1993 and January 1994 and was made up of 300 questionnaires and a total of 121 completed questionnaires were returned.

The results of the survey were added to the comparative analysis and categorization of member states in the Regulation Scale. The comparative analysis and initial categorization indicated both the subjectivity of the author with the objectivity of the data itself, that is, the legislation and subsequent regulatory structures. The survey results illustrate the subjectivity of the questions with the pursued objectivity of the respondents. These two sources compiled together attempt as objective an understanding as possible, of the member states' regulatory environments and what they wished of the developing SEM. The former approach provided a theoretical framework for analysis and related more to the constructivist approach. The latter part, or the survey, attempted to involve a level of reliability and was linked closer to a positivist perspective of theory. Indeed, by using both paradigms the study begins to mix methodological perspectives and theoretical frameworks. Different ontologies become apparent in that the former approach identified 'historical realism' through cultural change and the latter 'critical realism' through the pursuit of greater objectivity and control.

The results of the survey are listed below:

Question (a) investigated the level of regulation in each member state. Companies were asked to identify levels of regulation on a scale of 1–12. As with the comparative analysis, the responses were categorized into liberal, prescribed and state-controlled structures for the responding member states. The results of question (a) are summarized in Table 7.1.

The responses summarized in Table 7.1 were subsequently used to amend the scale (Figure 7.1). The means of the responses illustrated in Table 7.1 were averaged with the category assessment identified in Figure 7.1. This gave equal weight to both the initial categorization of the regulatory structures and perceptions of the life insurance industry. This led to marginal changes to the categorization of member state regulatory structures, indicating a degree of consistency between the two sources of data (see Figure 7.2).

Question (b) required companies to identify the EU regulatory structure at that moment in time (1993/94). This again was on a scale of 1–12 that categorized the regulatory environments as liberal, prescribed and state-controlled (the responses are summarized in Table 7.2).

Table 7.1 Perceived regulatory environment

	Liberal %	Prescribed %	State-controlled %	Mean	Categorization in Figure 7.1
United Kingdom	66.7	33.3	0.0	4	Liberal
Germany	4.0	52.0	44.0	8	Prescribed
Italy	0.0	66.7	33.3	8	S/controlled
The Netherlands	93.3	6.7	0.0	3	Liberal
France	12.6	18.8	67.8	8	S/controlled
Other	31.3	62.6	6.3	5	Lib/prescribed
All	38.1	40.5	21.5	6	N/A

Source: Howell (1999, 2000).

Table 7.2 EU regulatory structure

	Liberal %	Prescribed %	State-controlled %	Mean	Categorization in Figure 7.1
United Kingdom	13.9	69.5	16.7	6	Liberal
Germany	36.0	64.0	0.0	5	Prescribed
Italy	26.7	73.3	0.0	5	S/controlled
The Netherlands	35.7	64.3	0.0	5	Liberal
France	12.6	62.6	25.0	7	S/controlled
Other	25.0	68.8	6.3	6	Lib/prescribed
All	28.3	61.7	10.0	6	N/A

Source: Howell (1999, 2000).

Table 7.3 Most advantageous EU regulatory structure

	Liberal %	Prescribed %	State-controlled %	Mean	Categorization in Figure 7.1
United Kingdom	72.2	27.8	0.0	3	Liberal
Germany	32.0	68.0	0.0	6	Prescribed
Italy	66.7	33.4	0.0	4	S/controlled
The Netherlands	92.9	7.1	0.0	3	Liberal
France	29.4	70.6	0.0	6	S/controlled
Other	50.0	50.0	0.0	5	Lib/prescribed
All	58.3	41.7	0.0	4	N/A

Source: Howell (1999, 2000).

In general, there was agreement that the SEM was located between 5.0 and 7.0 with the mean of the responses equal to 6.0.

Question (c) required companies to indicate which type of regulatory structure would give them the greatest advantage in the evolving SEM. The results are summarized in Table 7.3. Generally, the member states pursued regulatory structures that were less regulated or similar to their own. However, there are differences between amounts of freedom that each state considered acceptable. This suggested that compromise could to be reached between the prescribed and liberal markets (such a compromise is shown in Figure 7.2).

Question (d) asked companies, which type of regulatory structure would allow the greatest consumer protection. Question (e) asked companies, which type of regulatory structure would allow the greatest consumer choice. Each of these enabled an understanding of what the respondents considered a regulatory structure should entail and gave insight into their perceptions in respect of the first three questions. Responses are summarized in Tables 7.4 and 7.5.

These responses suggested that there was a form of hegemony when it came to understanding the survey and the concept of a regulatory structure. However, this is more explicit in terms of the understanding of consumer choice. In the construction of EU directives in financial services it was around these very issues (the extent of interference regarding choice and protection) that the debates revolved. This is further illustrated in Chapter 8.

Table 7.4   Appropriate regulatory structure for consumer protection

	Liberal %	Prescribed %	State-controlled %	Mean	Categorization in Figure 7.1
United Kingdom	22.2	63.9	13.1	6	Liberal
Germany	20.0	56.0	24.0	7	Prescribed
Italy	50.0	50.0	0.0	5	S/controlled
The Netherlands	20.0	80.0	0.0	5	Liberal
France	11.8	52.9	35.3	7	S/controlled
Other	25.0	62.5	12.5	6	Lib/prescribed
All	30.8	53.3	15.8	6	N/A

Source: Howell (1999, 2000).

Table 7.5   Appropriate regulatory structure for consumer choice

	Liberal %	Prescribed %	State-controlled %	Mean	Categorization in Figure 7.1
United Kingdom	86.1	13.9	0.0	2	Liberal
Germany	96.0	4.0	0.0	2	Prescribed
Italy	83.3	16.7	0.0	4	S/controlled
The Netherlands	100.0	0.0	0.0	3	Liberal
France	70.6	17.7	11.8	4	S/controlled
Other	88.1	12.5	0.0	3	Lib/prescribed
All	87.6	10.5	1.7	3	N/A

Source: Howell (1999, 2000).

Conclusions

Through a comparative analysis of member state regulation, categorization and data accumulated through the survey, this chapter constructed a Regulation Scale. The analysis proposed that through the SEM, member states were forced into recognizing different regulatory structures and through compromise construct shared beliefs. However, this chapter also proposed that the normative concept of the SEM is tempered by the ideas, which the industries had of their own trading structures and that these differ from one member state to the next.

The state-controlled and greater prescribed environments indicated the convergence process with the greatest clarity as these structures were bringing their supervision into line with the less regulated markets. It would be these regulatory structures that would be open to the most intensive downloading (En1). However, the more liberal regulatory environments also needed to reform policies so as to bring them into line with European directives and downloading (En1). The less prescribed and less liberal markets have the fewest changes to make. This is particularly so for Belgium and the Republic of Ireland (Eire) and to a lesser extent Spain, Denmark, the United Kingdom and the Netherlands. The reason for this would be twofold; on the one hand, European integration defined the parameters of regulatory structure through insisting on opening up member state markets to ensure cross-border trade. On the other hand, member state industries were uploading preferences regarding the specifics of the regulatory structure and at least two of the state-controlled environments wanted to trade in more liberal structures. The state-controlled member state industries preferred less regulation on their trading structure. However, the Italians preferred a liberal environment, whereas at this point the French would have remained with one that was highly prescribed.

The United Kingdom and Dutch life insurance industries preferred more liberal structures than other member states, and one very similar to what is generally understood to be their home market conditions. In short, the liberal life industries wanted the new structure to be as similar to their own as possible; this would allow greater certainty and profitability. The prescribed markets preferred greater freedom but not to the extent that they would be put at a disadvantage.

The Regulation Scale and tables identified shared beliefs among member states. They indicated that compromise between the member states allows a directive to be formulated between 4.5 and 6.5 and that through mutual recognition and crossloading these points are integrated at the compromise convergence point (5–6 on the matrix) (see Figures 7.1 and 7.2). However, in initial negotiations, member states and national industries are generally looking for legislation and consequent regulation as similar to their own as possible, that is, the United Kingdom pursuing a 3 and Germany an 8. Through compromise and recognition of what the Commission perceives as necessary, shared beliefs are established (this will be discussed further in the following two chapters). This adds an impetus to European integration through 'recognition' in a European market and calls for harmonization in further areas. This illustrates cultivated and functional spillover to the extent that further legislation will be necessary in life insurance and other financial sectors, that is, banking and capital markets. It also illustrates the role of supranational institutions or European integration because the needs of the Commission and treaties are built into the legislation. No one single member state gets all of its own way: the legislation is both a compromise and one that reflects a European perspective. Uploading takes place and shared beliefs are reached, but the European integration process still has an important role to play before downloading takes place. The next chapter investigates this role and identifies the interaction between micro uploading and European integration through a study of supranational institutions and sub-national interests.

Each member state industry is used to trading in a distinct regulatory environment. This is in reference to both the formulation and eventual outcomes of regulations and directives. Considering the basic tenets of the treaties and competition policy compromise needed to take place between the prescribed and liberal regulation structures. Consequently, it was between these structures that shared beliefs were emerging and new regulation formed. However, even though shared beliefs were under construction interpretations of directives at the domestic level would be different and this would ensure levels of diversity.

8
Shared Beliefs and Micro and Macro Uploading

Introduction

This chapter builds on the data outlined in Chapter 7 and argues that sub-national interests play a central role in dealing with the difference in the formulation of shared beliefs. Indeed, sub-national interests provide the environment for the formulation of shared beliefs and the stimulation for micro En2 (sub-national uploading).

As noted in the previous chapter, separate member states had different regulatory structures based on historical and cultural heterogeneity. For instance, prior to the Single European Market (SEM) British financial service regulatory structures were relatively liberal in relation to other European Union (EU) member states, with supervision based on self-regulation. Other member states had different regulatory structures that ranged from state-controlled sectors like Greece, Portugal and Italy; highly regulated sectors like Germany and France, and more liberal sectors such as the Netherlands and Luxembourg. However, through the formulation of the SEM in financial services shared beliefs were realized regarding levels of regulation in the EU. In the 1980s, member states had different beliefs regarding supervision however, by the end of the 1990s, there was some convergence of these beliefs. Agreed legislation moved the regulatory structures away from self-regulation and state-control and identified a means by which shared beliefs could be realized in the evolving regulatory structure (for further see Howell, 1999, 2000, 2002, 2003).

This chapter identifies how supranational institutions through European integration processes interact with sub-national interests in legislation formulation. Sub-national interests are defined as governmental and non-governmental organizations (NGOs) that attempt to have an influence on public policy. They are entities that provide an institutional linkage between sectors and government (Kirchner, 1980). More precisely they are 'those types of organisations whose political task it is to reflect the interests of the economic or occupational sections they represent' (Lieber, 1974, p. 29). Sub-national interests can be described as 'organisations, which are occupied... in trying to influence the policy of public bodies in their own chosen direction... which represents either a number of similar groupings or both national groupings and European industry committee groupings' (Kirchner, 1980, p. 96). Sub-national interests upload sector preferences through the European Commission and Parliament, preferences, which through European integration procedures are eventually incorporated in policy-making mechanisms, for example directives and downloaded to member states.

Sub-national interests and micro uploading

The Single European Act (SEA) created an impetus for the involvement of sub-national interests in the EU policy-making process. With Qualified Majority Voting (QMV) and the SEM programme, lobbying in Brussels became imperative. 'European institutions (especially the European Commission and the European Parliament) have developed a comprehensive network of contacts that cut across, and are independent of, member countries. Increasingly it is necessary for lobbying to be based on broad alliances representing a more European perspective. We might think of this process as Europeanization' (Andersen and Eliassen, 1991, p. 174 author's brackets). Through the use of national interest groups, European-wide interest groups, large companies and networks sector preferences are uploaded into the European integration domain or European political space. In this way we observe an interaction between Europeanization and European integration in the formulation of policy. When formulating financial services policy the European Commission attempts to involve all sub-national interests. However, the European Commission preferred to deal with European-wide interest groups because these provided a European perspective.

European-wide interest groups and supranational institutions make it impossible for one member state to be purely self-interested. Domestic self-interest has become intermeshed with other member states; 'national self-interest has partly become a collective European interest ... forty years of working together has resulted in collective outputs being produced and recognised by the parties involved' (Greenwood, 1995, p. 2). If common interests are to exist then they must be based on a set of shared beliefs. The European Commission and Parliament consider that speaking to European organizations allows an understanding of European-wide interests or the shared beliefs of European sectors. Indeed, to ensure effective lobbying it is necessary to build coalitions. At the same time, both the European Commission and the European Parliament stressed that they wanted to speak to European-wide institutions because this provided shared beliefs and European rather than domestic or company perspectives. This may be made a little clearer through a study of financial services, in general, and the Third Life Assurance Directive, in particular.

Formulating shared beliefs: micro uploading and European integration

Most financial services companies are members of interest groups and use these to influence UK policy-making. For instance, in a survey of UK life insurance companies 100 per cent of respondents subscribed to a national interest group and most of these were members of the Association of British Insurers (ABI) (Howell, 1999, 2000). Indeed, through their membership of the ABI they were automatically part of a European-wide interest group; the Comité Européen des Assurances (CEA).

Insurance interest representation at the EU level is primarily undertaken by the CEA, which has operated throughout Europe since 1953. The institution existed before the creation of the European Economic Community (EEC) and this is reflected in its membership, which it is not made up of member states alone. 'Nevertheless the single most important function of the organisation is to work through its "Common Market Committee", which is officially recognised by the EU and through which all insurance directives pass' (Vipond, 1995, p. 105). This perception is also reflected by the European Commission, which considered itself as an organization that is always open to and welcomes external input; input, which can be seen as uploading. The Commission has 'a reputation for being accessible to interest groups [because] it is in the Commission's own interest to do so since interest groups can provide the services with technical information and constructive advice' (OJ/C 63/02).

Directorate-Generale XV (DG XV) considered the CEA to be the main representative of the insurance industry sentiments, which were reinforced in a speech by Leon Brittan in 1989 'the CEA has proved its worth... as a standard bearer for the insurance industry at the European level. I know that DG XV has come to rely greatly on the CEA and its officials... as an organisation which is fully representative of the insurance industry, which puts your views and concerns to us frankly and powerfully and defends them tenaciously' (Sir Leon Brittan, speech given to the CEA November 1989, cited in Camerra-Rowe, 1996, p. 18). These sentiments were supported by a number of interviews undertaken by Howell (1999, 2000), Mazey and Richardson (1993) and Camerra-Rowe (1996) in which a Commission official indicated 'they [the Commission] have almost institutionalised corporatist – like relations with the CEA' (p. 18).

Investigating micro uploading: a summary of interviews

A set of interviews, undertaken in the early 1990s, identified the relationships between sub-national, national and supranational interests in the insurance industry (see Howell, 1999, 2000) (a summary of the interviews are reported here).

The key individuals interviewed by the author were representatives of the following institutions.

Directorate-Generale XV (DG XV).
The Council of Ministers Permanent Representative for UK.
The Department of Industry and Trade (DTI). ·
Committee for European Assurance (CEA), Paris and Brussels.
Bureau International des Producteurs d'Assurance & de Reassurance (BIPAR).
Association of British Insurers (ABI).
British Insurers International Committee (BIIC).

Irish Insurance Federation (IIF).
Council of Ministers Permanent Representative for France.

Salient points identified through the interview programme included evidence that DG XV primarily dealt with European-wide sub-national interests and that the initial call for legislation may come through the member state government, sector or European Commission. In this way, the starting point of regulatory reform can be macro/micro En2, En3 or European integration.

In the previous chapter, categorization and the survey identified differentiation regarding member state regulation structures. The interview programme indicated that the CEA saw its role, as bringing together a combined understanding of the direction that the negotiations should take: the CEA provided the basis or environment for shared beliefs to be formulated. Furthermore, the CEA, BIPAR and DG XV representatives all considered that the Commission preferred to deal with a European-wide interest group. Once shared beliefs have been reached between national interest groups the European-wide interest group acted as uploader. The ABI and BIIC were members of and worked through the CEA. Following the SEA it was easier to develop shared beliefs in a European-wide organization in conjunction with the European Commission. Consequently, the importance of the CEA has continued to grow. Once shared beliefs had been developed the BIIC and ABI relayed common understandings to the national government.

During attempts to formulate shared beliefs DG XV members negotiate with member state interest groups, for example the ABI or directly with companies. But its main contacts are the European interest groups because they provide a European perspective. European interest groups formulate the basis of shared beliefs among its membership and this ensures acceptable compromise and successful directives.

For example, CEA representatives argued that they played an interactive and important part in the creation of European legislation, as did those representatives of the ABI, BIIC and BIPAR. Extensive uploading is undertaken by business associations who ensure that their influence is part of the negotiations as early as possible. Overall, interest groups are an intrinsic element in the process of negotiation. Ultimately, the CEA is an important micro uploader in the formulation of negotiations because it provides an all-round or complete perspective of the sector's demands from the policy-making institutions. Moreover, CEA agents perceived themselves as facilitators and like the Commission representatives argued that European-wide interest groups provided the means by which a European perspective and shared beliefs and this enabled successful legislation.

In general, each interviewee agreed that different member states initially pursued conflicting regulatory structures. A CEA representative argued that member states had different ideas about what was the most appropriate regulatory structure and that this was due to differing normative and historical experiences. Overall interviewees supported the data in Chapter 7 that identified different understandings of regulatory structures and that European-wide interest groups were a necessary element in bringing about shared beliefs.

Developing shared beliefs through micro uploading

In late the 1980s, sub-national interests became more aware of what was necessary if they were to participate in the development of EU legislation. Of course, there are a number of difficulties in continually reaching agreement and member groupings and companies attempted to influence the policy-making institutions themselves (see Chapter 6, Coen, 1997, 1998 and Howell, 2000). However, the European policy-making institutions made it clear that negotiations should be undertaken through the CEA or other European interest groups. The CEA interacts with many other groups at the EU level, for example banking employers groups and trade unions. Indeed, the CEA attempted to become part of the policy-making process as early as possible and to this extent it had a good relationship with DG XV. In this way the CEA is an important micro uploader in EU policy-making.

There were close and consistent interactions between the member state industries and European institutions. Compromise was reached at the European interest-group level through negotiations between national interest groups and EU policy-making institutions. Proposed legislation that goes through to the Council of Ministers incorporates shared beliefs of the majority of member states' national interest groups who then inform their own government of these common beliefs. This indicates elements of neo-functionalism and a multilevel governance approach. However, during the process there may be disagreements between the Council of Ministers and the other institutions. This identified an interaction between neo-functionalism and intergovernmentalism and provided an example of multilevel rather than state-centric governance. Indeed, micro uploading identified a specific aspect of neo-functionalism (interest groups turning towards another policy-making institution) and macro uploading an element of intergovernmentalism (national preferences).

National interest groups upload domestic preferences to the European interest group; European interest groups provide an environment in which different beliefs can be explored and developed into shared beliefs regarding the structure of the evolving SEM (of course, differences still remain but a consistent approach is reached). Shared beliefs are eventually compromised with those pursued by the EU for instance in interviews, DG XV representatives considered that they pursued 'the spirit of the treaties' in their negotiations with interest groupings (Howell, 2000). Through this process a regulatory structure is eventually agreed and downloaded through the EU and domestic policy-making structures. However, the level of convergence throughout the EU will be tempered (especially with regard to directives) through domestic cultures and identities having an impact on interpretations of downloaded policy. Overall, through interest intermediation common discourse can evolve which paves the way or provides the basis for vertical policy transfer (VPT/En3). As noted in Chapter 3, VPT came through EU policy or European integration processes. horizontal policy transfer (HPT) incorporated learning from and taking on other member state policies with limited EU involvement. One may argue that HPT does not incorporate En3 because change does not emanate through EU structures and it is not affected by European integration. However (as noted in Chapter 3) there are problems with this distinction, for example member states may learn from other member states who have themselves made changes because of VPT. In other words, it may affect European integration. Through an analysis of the financial services sector in relation to uploading (En2), downloading (En1), crossloading (En3) and European integration the rest of this chapter deals with some of these issues.

Spillover, financial services and European integration theory

As noted in Chapters 2 and 3, supranationality, sub-national interests and spillover (cultivated, institutional and functional) are central to neo-functionalism. Institutional spillover can be identified as a means by which treaties generate policy issue extensions that impact on and can be cultivated by EU institutions. Functional spillover is apparent when co-operation in one sector expands into another. Legislation in one sector creates the need for legislation in other sectors and/or further legislation in different areas of the same sector. In this context, the establishment of a SEM incorporated institutional cultivated and functional spillover, for example in institutional terms it necessitated further powers for supranational institutions whereby further integration could be cultivated through closer involvement in uploading procedures. Functional spillover indicated what Haas (1958) labelled the 'expansive logic of sector integration' which through a variety of sectors swapping concessions indicated the motor of European integration (p. 243).

This chapter considers that macro uploading provides the foundations for spillover that 'successful spillover requires prior programmatic agreement expressed in an intergovernmental bargain' (p. 287). That macro uploading also involves the pursuit of national preferences and consequently involves intergovernmental procedures. Once macro uploading and European integration has developed treaties and policy programmes, micro uploading through sub-national interests involve themselves in the process through EU channels and add an impetus to functional spillover.

In the 1980s, domestic policy positions regarding further integration were changing. For instance, the United Kingdom pursued deregulation, France changed its economic policy, Spain wanted economic modernization and Germany wished for monetary stability. Each was changing policy in relation to global competitive pressures (primarily from the United States and Japan) and internal pressures that called for a true common market and cross-border trade in the EEC. For instance when Margaret Thatcher was asked in 1989 why she had agreed to the SEA she argued that the United Kingdom 'wished to have many of the directives under majority voting because things which we wanted were being stopped by others using a single vote. For instance, we have not yet got insurance as freely in Germany as we wished' (cited in Keohane and Hoffman, 1990, p. 287). However, according to Haas major changes in European integration and spillover depend on both self-interest and shared beliefs. On a macro level, in the 1950s and 1960s these shared beliefs revolved around Keynesian economic policies and in the 1980s and early 1990s around deregulation or re-regulation. This chapter illustrates the latter changes on a micro level and through the development of sector-wide shared beliefs recognition of a common interest.

Functional spillover may be observed in individual industries, that is within the insurance industry or banking industry as well as in financial services in general, that is between insurance, banking, pensions and so on. Institutional spillover may be observed in the impact the treaties have on supranational institutions, which is then cultivated further within these institutions. Indeed, 'spillover requires prior programmatic agreement among governments, expressed in an intergovernmental bargain. Such a bargain is clearly important in accounting for the Single European Act' (Keohane and Hoffman, 1991, p. 17). Institutional spillover provided the environment for further functional spillover to take place and identified further interactions between sub-national interests and supranational institutions between micro En2 and European integration processes.

The liberalization of insurance and banking is tied closely to the free movements of capital. Indeed, the treaties stipulate that the liberalization of the banking and insurance sectors 'shall be effected in step with the progressive liberalisation of the movement of capital' (Foster, 1999, p. 14, Art. 51 (I) ex Art. 61). This could be seen as an example of institutional spillover providing the initial impetus for further functional spillover. Or one may consider that this type of article provided a functional area within the Treaty, which defines the scope of integration. As numerous actors become involved in policy-making at different levels and intensity, Europeanization in terms of uploading can be identified. European integration in terms of the treaties and institutional development is a reaction to macro uploading and the interactions between the domestic and EU levels that this creates. The development of policy mechanisms to be downloaded is primarily achieved through micro uploading and European integration procedures. Each of these areas provides impetus for functional spillover in the form of downloading.

Functional spillover and downloading directives

Insurance legislation can provide examples of downloading and functional spillover. For example, initially there were two general programmes proposed to ensure that both freedom of services and establishment would be realized in life insurance by the beginning of 1970. In line with the Economic and Monetary Union (EMU), insurance was to be integrated and legislation downloaded in the following way:

1964 Reinsurance. Freedom of establishment and services.
1966 Indemnity insurance. Freedom of establishment.
1968 Life insurance. Freedom of establishment.
1968 Indemnity insurance. Freedom of services.
1970 Life insurance. Freedom of services.

However, international and internal pressures did not demand En1 and institutional spillover or the necessary political will and environment for adherence to this timetable. There was no macro uploading from member states regarding the programme and limited opportunity at the EU level for policy development and En1. Between the 1980s and 1990s, international competitive pressures on member states gradually changed their perspectives. As noted above, through changes in domestic policy objectives macro uploading developed institutional spillover and provided the environment for functional spillover and the realization of an SEM. During the 1980s, macro uploading realized institutional spillover in the SEA, QMV and co-operation procedure, and in the 1990s the Maastricht Treaty and co-decision procedures and EMU. Through macro uploading the foundations for intensified micro uploading were laid.

In the proposal for the Third Life Assurance Directive, the European Commission emphasized that 'the internal market in insurance represents a primary goal...in view of the importance of this strongly expanding sector'.[1] The insurance industry considered that it needed priority treatment because it lagged behind in the liberalization of the other economic sectors within the financial services sector. Directives in securities and banking had already been implemented and as a consequence the insurance industry had been left at a competitive disadvantage. These concerns identify explicit examples of En1 and functional spillover.

In insurance, En1 has taken form in three generations of directives dating from the late 1970s. The life assurance directives illustrate functional spillover with each generation creating the need for the next. Each new generation that was downloaded created the need for further legislation, both in other areas of insurance and financial services in general and provided an impetus for further uploading, European integration, downloading and crossloading.

Directive (91/675/EEC) formed the Insurance Committee to act as an intermediary between the industry (sub-national interests) and the Commission and to assist in implementation procedures. The Committee also examines any questions relating to the application of existing directives and the preparation of new legislation proposals in the insurance industry. This could be seen as an example of spillover and supranationality interacting with each other (Kirchner, 1976; Tranholm-Mikkelsen, 1991). It also obscures the distinction between, uploading and European integration on the one hand, and European integration and downloading on the other. Indeed, the Insurance Committee provided a forum for uploaded preferences to be discussed on a technical level and like the Banking Advisory Committee (BAC), indicated the close proximity and blurred edges between En2 and European integration. Furthermore, once we investigate the role of the Insurance Committee in the development of policy and where it fits within the model we must also question the European interest group. Is this a part of En2 or European integration? Indeed, these difficulties illustrate the problems encountered when attempting to differentiate between Europeanization and European integration while at the same time explaining the interaction as 'process'. In attempting to create a European market in insurance further directives were and are necessary and even though extensive downloading has taken place further harmonization is required. Each piece of legislation necessitated and created the basis of the next. This downloading has formed the basis of the regulatory structure and provides an illustration of functional spillover.

Downloading directives: constructing an SEM in financial services

George (2001) argued that downloading or En1 was the clearest example of Europeanization. This may be observed in the financial services sector in the context of two co-ordination directives that have primarily affected the European banking industry. The First Banking Directive (77/780/EEC) cleared many obstacles to the freedom of establishment for banks and other credit institutions, introduced home country supervision (supervision by domestic regulators) and a common position for the granting of banking licences. However, problems were still apparent and certain obstacles needed to be removed before a genuine single market in banking could be achieved. Member states lobbied for further integration through uploading or En2 and established further directives in the quest for a single market in financial services. The Second Banking Directive (89/646/EEC) aimed for the removal of authorization problems, that is differentials in supervisory rules and structures and definitions of banking activities and cross-border trade. It enabled a single banking licence; a list of banking activities and minimum capital levels (5 m ECU, now euros, laid down for new banks). The Second Banking Directive also provided supervisory rules in terms of internal management, audit systems and control levels of major shareholders. Furthermore, once banks could trade cross-border, other credit institutions lobbied for a level playing field in financial services. This illustrates a loop back in the process with downloading in one industry bringing about uploading in another. For instance, as stated earlier, the insurance industry considered that it needed priority treatment because it lagged behind the liberalization of the other economic sectors within the financial services sector. The banking directives left the insurance industry at a disadvantage so it pressed for equitability at the domestic and EU levels (an example of up-loading (En2) to the EU policy-making institutions and further spillover).

Furthermore, following the banking directives and insurance directives, other financial services providers felt they were at a disadvantage and further change was sought. Such led to the directive on Investment Firms and Credit Institutions (CAD), which provided the framework for the Investment Services Directive (ISD) (93/22/EEC) both directives attempted to create an internal market in investment services and give all institutions, whether credit or investment firms, the ability to offer investment services throughout the EU.

In other parts of the sector, the interaction between En1, En2, En3 and European integration took place regarding the formulation and implementation of the Co-Insurance Directive (78/473/EEC), the

Credit and Surety ship Assurance Directive amending Directive (87/343/EEC), the Legal Expenses Directive (87/344/EEC) and the Council Directive on the Annual Accounts and Consolidated Accounts of Insurance Undertakings (AACAIU) (91/674/EEC).

The AACAIU proposal regarding harmonization of EU insurance accounting practices, which would be necessary if valuation and solvency indicators were to be uniform, provided an example of downloading. Also under discussion during the early 1990s was the proposal for a Council directive on the co-ordination of laws, regulations and administrative provisions relating to insurance contracts. This was discontinued in 1993 following the idea of the general good. This is where member states can protect consumers through abjuring certain products from their territories. Initially, one might argue that in this context En2 was unsuccessful because the European integration process was unable to provide shared beliefs and compromise. However, 'general good' does involve shared beliefs in the context of four stringent tests:

(a) Public interest test = public interest reasons that justify restrictions;
(b) Duplication test = public interest is not protected in member state where providers are established;
(c) Non-discriminatory test = applies to all;
(d) Proportionality test = the same result cannot be obtained from less restrictive regulation.

'General good' intends to provide balance between public interest of consumers in individual member states and the creation of an SEM in insurance. Fundamentally, to ensure the judicial application of these tests clear demarcations regarding 'competent authorities' and their responsibilities are necessary in all member states.

In this way, directives may only partially regulate cross-border activity. On the one hand, En2 and European integration encourage shared beliefs and EU directives. On the other hand, diverse domestic interpretation of En1 ensures differentiation that may be used as barriers between member states. However, En3 through VPT and mutual recognition or further En2 may deal with these discrepancies; if they do not then the concept of 'general good' may be used by member states to keep certain products out of domestic markets.

In this context, 'general good' identified the necessity of clear demarcation regarding the role of 'competent authorities' throughout the EU. The directives indicate that 'competent authorities' should regulate financial services products and activities and ensure consumer protection. As member states must allow financial service companies supervised by other 'competent authorities' to trade in their territories, and interpret 'general good', there needs to be a high level of clarity and confidence regarding regulatory institutions. As recognition between 'competent authorities' evolve, 'general good' becomes less necessary. As confidence between member state regulators emerges there should be less need to evoke what could be seen as a barrier to trade. Furthermore, the implementation of the EC Unfair Contract Terms Directive in 1993 reduced the extent that insurance contracts could be used as Non-Tariff Barriers (NTBs). However, member states found difficulty in reaching a compromise in these areas because of sovereignty, cultural and market structure issues.

Overall, banking legislation and its consequent regulation necessitates regulation in other financial services industries. This process is illustrated by the interaction between security markets, insurance and banking. Indeed, one may consider that this is an example of uploading by the individual industries to the EU and European integration and ultimately downloading to the member states through directives. This may be made a little clearer through a study of the Third Life Assurance Directive and the notion of a competent authority.

Downloading shared beliefs: a competent authority

As identified in the summary of interviews earlier, the ABI and CEA were highly involved in the creation of the Third Life Assurance Directive. The ABI forwarded a policy of self-regulation, which was partially taken up by the CEA and DG XV but eventually led to a more specific concept of 'competent authority' and a less liberal regulatory structure than the UK life insurance industry would have preferred.

The Third Life Insurance Directive identified that the 'competent authority' should introduce appropriate safeguards to prevent 'irregularities and infringements of the provisions of assurance supervision' (OJ 360; Art., 10). Furthermore, the Third Life Insurance Directive indicated that member states must have an institution capable of ensuring the 'orderly pursuit of business by insurance undertakings' (ibid.). Through the SEM, consumers should have wider choice; however, they must be provided with enough information to enable choices best suited to their needs. Such information is all the more important when the contract is of a long-term nature. Consequently, the consumer should receive clear and accurate information regarding the 'essential character of the products proposed' (ibid., Art., 23) and an accurately defined complaints procedure. The Second Banking Directive indicated that the 'competent authority' for credit institutions should provide authorization in terms of capital as well as sound prudent management (Art. 5). Given the problems regarding misselling in the UK financial services sector and difficulties regarding competencies in the regulatory structure these stipulations could not have been achieved by the structure that existed in the early 1990s and some change would be necessary if the directive was to be fully downloaded. The level of change and the type of structure was at this point open to interpretation, which illustrated the diversity still apparent in applying directives. Indeed, member states pursued different models of regulatory structure, elements of which still exist today.

The Third Life Insurance Directive identified what a regulated market should involve. It included regulations approved by the appropriate 'competent authorities', which should be empowered by national authorities to supervise insurance undertakings. Furthermore, the 'competent authorities' may also restrict authorization of both companies and products (Art. 4). So when the Financial Services Authority (FSA) gives authorization for classes of insurance or companies, it is valid for the entire EU (except in the context of general good). 'Competent authorities' encompass member state authorities that are statutorily empowered to supervise insurance undertakings and are able to grant and withhold authorization. The 'competent authority' should ensure minimum guarantees and that reputable individuals control and administer companies. It should also carry out verification and authorization of a company's ability to trade in other member states (this may be accomplished with the assistance of the member state authority in which the company trades) (Arts 5 and 9). However, the

> financial supervision of an assurance undertakings ... shall be the sole responsibility of the home member state. If the 'competent authorities' of the member state of the commitment have reason to consider that the activities of an assurance undertaking might affect its financial soundness, they should inform the competent

authorities of the home member state. The latter authorities shall determine whether the undertaking is complying with the prudential principles laid down in this Directive. (Art. 8, Para. 1)

Supervision incorporated levels of solvency, and technical provisions, both mathematical and assets covering these provisions in relation to regulations indicated by the member state based on principles outlined in the directive. Overall, the 'competent authorities ... shall require every assurance undertaking to have sound administrative and accounting procedures and adequate internal control mechanisms' (Art. 8, Para. 3).

Each member state will need to ensure that its competent authority is able to carry out the supervision of companies with head offices in their territories, which includes business in other member states. The competent authority must have the powers to ensure that council directives are implemented. In a practical context, this means the ability to investigate an undertaking in terms of all of its business on the spot and insist on documentation being made available. The competent authority also needs to ensure consumer protection in all member states and have the means of enforcement at its disposal. It may also make provision for the 'competent authorities to obtain any information regarding contracts which are held by intermediaries' (Art. 10, Para. C).

Conclusions

In general, shared beliefs and compromise are achieved at the European interest-group level through negotiations with the European Commission and European Parliament. If legislation is being negotiated through sub-national interests interacting with supranational institutions (EU policy-makers) the research has identified an example of neo-functionalism. In achieving successful acceptable legislation at the EU level, both neofunctional and inter-governmental processes, in the form of multilevel governance are identifiable.

The EU insurance industry uses interest groups at the EU level to serve both the self-interest of its membership (the national industries through national interest groups) and the collective interest of the EU industry as a whole when faced with an evolving SEM. The CEA is made up of national interest groups, which allows easier compromise in the EU domain. This ensures further European integration in insurance and other financial services industries.

If member state industries/sectors are involved in the creation of European legislation, other industries/sectors through self-interest/common interest are drawn into the process. This is identifiable in the interaction between the insurance and banking industries. However, to allow functional spillover to take place (as indicated by attempts in the 1970s to create an SEM in insurance) intergovernmental treaties through institutional spillover must ensure the necessary environment, for example the Single European Act and the SEM and the Maastricht Treaty and EMU.

Following macro uploading and the shared belief between member states that an SEM was necessary, domestic and European interest groups micro uploaded preferences to EU policy-making institutions, which through European integration processes formulated legislation that was then downloaded to member states. In this context, we can observe the formulation of directives (through micro uploading and European integration) in banking, insurance and capital markets. These directives and regulations are then downloaded to member states where different interpretations of policies are implemented. Unification does take place but there is room for cultural diversity. Furthermore, believing the drive towards a single market in financial services had faltered there was further macro uploading of shared beliefs by member state governments and through this uploading and European integration processes the Financial Services Action Plan (FSAP) was formulated (in this way we observe an interaction between macro uploading and European integration). The following chapters in this section identify macro uploading in the late 1990s and the early twenty-first century and downloading and crossloading in relation to the United Kingdom, Germany, Poland and Italy.

9
Macro Uploading and Supranational Institutions: Formulating the Financial Services Action Plan (FSAP)

Introduction

The Economic and Monetary Union (EMU) intensified the rationale for an integrated financial services sector. Research conducted for the European Commission identified significant benefits for consumers, businesses and investors. This indicated that EU-wide Gross Domestic Product (GDP) will increase by 1.1 per cent or €130b at 2002 prices over 10–15 years. Employment will increase by 0.5 per cent and integrated equity markets will reduce the price of equity capital by 0.5 per cent with corporate bond finance falling by 0.4 per cent. Given these savings the EU and member states have stepped up their activities in their pursuit of a single market in financial services over the last five years. Indeed, following macro uploading and European integration procedures the Financial Services Action Plan (FSAP) provided the basis for further micro uploading, discussion and debate, and the eventual downloading of EU legislation into domestic domains.

The FSAP was based on the 'Financial Services: a Framework for Action' and following, its first meeting in January 1999, the outcomes of discussions by the Financial Services Policy Group (FSPG). The FSPG was set up 'to give new impetus to ensuring a fully functional single market for financial services' (European Commission, 1999a, p. 1). Indeed, the FSPG was put in place to 'forge consensus between national ministries involved in financial services regulation' (European Commission, 1999b, p. 1). Furthermore, 'forum groups' made up of financial services experts advised on technical implications of FSAP activities, problems etc. (European Commission, 1999c).

The Framework for Action and FSAP outlined the way forward if an improved single market in financial services was to be achieved and informed the discussions of member state representatives of the FSPG. Areas outlined by the Framework for Action involved wholesale markets, retail financial markets, supervisory co-operation and taxation. The FSAP incorporated these issues and concentrated on 'ensuring deep and liquid European capital markets, which serve both issuers and investors better and the removal of remaining barriers to cross-border provision in order to ensure consumer choice while maintaining consumer confidence and a high level of consumer protection' (European Commission, 1998, p. 1). The European Commission thought that in general the EU framework of prudential rules was acceptable. However, application of legislation needed to be more flexible so that prudential rules could adapt more easily to the evolving markets. Based on the European Commission's conclusions outlined in the Framework for Action and FSAP, the FSPG was requested to look at specific areas regarding the completion of the market and more flexible regulation (these are outlined in more detail here).

The FSAP: macro uploading and European integration

Romano Prodi, the President of the European Commission, argued that 'implementation of the FSAP must not be allowed to falter or fail'. He considered that such failure would impact on the EU strategy for 'sustainable growth, competitiveness, stability, employment and innovation' (cited in European Commission, 2002, p. 1). As noted in Chapter 5, financial services integration became an imperative following the launch of monetary union. The FSAP provided the opportunity for market expansion, cheaper finance and better value for consumers. There was a new understanding of the benefit that a single market in financial services could offer. Consequently, the FSAP was to target a number of areas where impediments to cross-border trade existed and harmonization was necessary. In total there were 42 measures to be dealt with which included:

(a) The completion of a single wholesale market. Issues to be dealt with under this heading involved barriers to raising capital, integrating securities and derivative markets, amendments to the Investment

Services Directive (ISD), amendments to company law directives, ensuring security and transparency for cross-border security trades and takeover bids, prudent supervision of tax arrangements for supplementary pensions.

(b) The development of open secure markets in retail financial services. With the development of e-commerce and other methods of distance selling, the FSAP wanted to remove obstacles relating to cross-border purchasing of financial services. Issues to be dealt with involved a directive on distance selling, and areas like transparency, security and mortgage credit information and a proposal for a directive on insurance intermediaries. Further consumer protection should also be introduced.

(c) Continuity of stability of EU financial markets. Financial regulation needed to keep pace with changes in risk and ensure flexible supervision to deal with systemic or institutional risk. Measures included: taking account of the Basel Accords and the institutionalization of the Forum of European Securities Commissions (FESCO). The proposal and adoption of directives regarding prudential legislation in terms of the liquidation of banks and insurance companies, electronic money, money laundering and solvency margins.

(d) Eliminate tax barriers to financial market integration. The FSAP emphasized the need to adopt the proposed directive on minimum effective taxation of cross-border income from savings and implementation of the code of conduct on business taxation. The Commission would also investigate, in conjunction with the Taxation Policy Group (TPG), and identify means of removing tax differences on cross-border insurance and pension products and coordinate tax arrangements concerning supplementary pensions (European Commission, 1999b).

European Commission (1999c) identified progress with the FSAP in a number of areas in terms of discussion and intention and indicated the need for greater effort in areas such as takeover bids and winding up. However, the overall assessment was that the FSAP had given a new impetus and urgency to the development of a single market in financial services. Frits Bolkestein the Internal Market Commissioner considered that the FSAP had been an important factor 'in pulling together all the strands necessary for the creation of a fully integrated internal market in financial services' (cited in European Commission,

2000, p. 1). European Commission (2000) outlined five new priorities for the FSAP relating to: financial statement comparability in the EU, barriers to pension fund investments and Undertakings for Collective Investments in Transferable Securities (UCITS), a major overhaul of the ISD, improvements in cross-border sale and repurchase markets and a single passport for issuers of equity. European Commission (2000) raised the stakes further when it called for intensified implementation of the FSAP, and extended priorities to a list of ten for the European Commission, the Council of Ministers and European Parliament. Areas specific to the Commission included: proposals for changes to prospectuses, market manipulation, cross-border use of collateral, prudential rules for financial conglomerates and capital framework governance for banks and investment firms directives and communications regarding accounting strategy, the ISD, business rules and e-commerce. The Commission also proposed to set up FESCO.

The ten priorities for the European Parliament and Council of Ministers involved: directives regarding, pension fund supervision, investment funds (UCITS), company statutes, takeover bids, distant marketing, liquidation of insurance companies, winding up of banks, savings tax, amendments to money laundering and the implementation of the 1997 conduct on business taxation. As requested by the Council of Finance Ministers, the European Commission charted a critical path to speed up adoption of these matters, this was undertaken by an informal group of representatives from the Council of Ministers and European Parliament who indicated problems with work schedules, avoided delays and speeded up formal procedures. However, European Commission (2001) urged for more concerted effort from the Council of Ministers and European Parliament in meeting targets as 'progress … has been broadly satisfactory but not sufficient' (p. 1). The Anti-Money Laundering Directive had been adopted, as had the European Company Statute Directive and there had been agreement on the Distant Marketing Directive. Furthermore, following proposals by the Lamfalussy Report regarding a committee for securities, FESCO was eventually established. Areas requiring more effort included prospectuses, pension funds, takeover bids, financial conglomerates and accounting standards. In all of the 42 measures set out in the FSAP 25 had been dealt with by 2002.

The UK Financial Services Authority (FSA) argued that the FSAP could be speeded up through tighter deadlines, and the utilization of expertise, improvements regarding the way directives are constructed and implemented and through consistency among member states. Insurance and banking committees assist in this process but such is not the case for securities. However, as noted, FESCO is now operating and has already proposed a set of principles to underpin a regulated securities market. It has suggested that a framework directive should indicate a single competent authority in each member state, which through delegation to FESCO advise on rules and regulations identified in directives and means of enforcement. Finally, mutual recognition needed to be better implemented if a fully functioning SEM in financial services was to be achieved.

The FSPG: macro uploading or European integration?

The FSPG was chaired by Commissioner Mario Monti and consisted of representatives of member state Finance Ministries, the European Central Bank (ECB), the European Commission and the Council of the European Union. Member state representation illustrated the domestic commitment to the development of a single market in financial services. 'The single market for financial services is crucial to the success of the euro and Economic and monetary Union' (European Commission, 1999, p. 1). At the first meeting of the FSPG Mario Monti argued that the membership needed to work collectively with an open mind so as to improve cross-border services and ensure consumer confidence. Furthermore, costs of small value cross-border payments and corporate governance principles which effect investment decisions needed particular attention (ibid.).

The immediate priorities for the FSPG were to work towards agreement on existing proposals, particularly those regarding the liquidation of banks and insurance companies, takeover bids and a European company statute. Furthermore, the FSPG was asked to affirm commitment to proposed Directives on UCITS, electronic money and distance selling so as to allow the Council to come to a common position by mid-1999. The FSPG was also asked to look at the improvement of existing legislation and prudential rules and regulations in terms of money laundering, listing prospectuses, and supervisory standards regarding banking, insurance, financial conglomerates, corporate governance and accounting and auditing. For instance the EU capital regime no longer captures the risks banks are undertaking or solvency requirements for long-term risk in insurance. With regard to financial conglomerates the FSPG was required to assess the supervision of risks run by these institutions. First, it is difficult to assess the overall risk of large conglomerates, consequently they may not be adequately addressed by any of the supervisors involved. Second, because these groups are so large financial difficulties may impact on the financial system in general.

On the one hand, the FSPG is requested to 'confirm that every effort should be made to update the Union's banking supervisory standards' but at the same time the Banking Advisory Committee (BAC) had already started to 'identify and remedy shortcomings in the rules' (ibid., p. 3). This illustrated the interaction between En2 and European integration. On the one hand, domestic confirmation and input is uploaded through the FSPG to the EU level whereas, on the other, the shortcomings and solutions are identified by the BAC at the EU level through European integration processes. In other words, uploading from the domestic level is apparent as member states agree/disagree regarding the development of EU legislation. However, the EU is proactive in defining the difficulties that need solutions, which identifies the area of policy change and the consequent solutions that may be uploaded. The idea for the framework for action was generated by the Vienna summit and at the European Council meeting in Cardiff (1998) the European Commission was invited to prepare a framework for action for financial services. Indeed, the main impetus for intensified change in financial services had come about through the implementation of EMU and builds on previous attempts at developing a single market in financial services.

A number of issues faced member states and the EU in their negotiations regarding the development of a deeper and wider SEM in financial services. If further cross-border trade was to be realized a number of difficulties needed to be overcome; for instance what should be the balance between competition, innovation and consumer protection? If regulation drives business offshore it may negate consumer benefit. To what extent should market integrity be promoted even though it had costs for borrowers and lenders? Of course, the answers to these questions would be different for individual member states and depend on the sophistication of individual financial systems and emphasizes that member states will implement different interpretations of EU policy. However, implementation should be in line with the parameters of EU policy. Some member states have been failing to implement or approve laws in financial services and such considerations motivated the British government to support claims by the European Commission that it needed more powers to force rogue member states to implement EU policy.

In 1999, for instance, Italy, Spain, Austria, Luxembourg and France were referred to the European Court of Justice (ECJ) because they failed to download EU financial services directives. For instance, Italy failed to implement a directive on the supervision of financial institutions; Spain imposed unfair requirements on insurance brokers from other member states; and Austria, France and Luxembourg failed to implement a directive on investor compensation schemes. Consequently, in some instances downloading has not taken place even though new legislation has been agreed at the EU level. Furthermore, in January 2001, the European Commission thought that nine member states had failed to implement legislation regarding capital requirements covering unforeseen risk.

The Commission argued that without an extension of its powers the SEM would miss its target and fail to become the most competitive economy in the world by 2010 (*Financial Times*, 2003, p. 8). Indeed, if Brussels were provided with more powers to enforce EU policy implementation, downloading and uploading would intensify and diversity would be limited. Furthermore, the FSAP also identified many concerns outlined by the FSA, in such a way attempts at policy transfer regarding the structure of the SEM had been taken up in areas of micro and macro uploading through the FSPG.

Discussions in the FSPG on the Framework for Action and FSAP identified five main areas where action was necessary to further facilitate the construction of a single market in financial services. These were: an improved legislative apparatus, elimination of capital market fragmentation, consumer protection within a single market, supervisory co-ordination, and an integrated infrastructure to underpin financial transactions. The European Commission (1998) concentrated on a number of main concerns regarding the European financial services market. These included, deep and liquid capital markets, which improve services to both issuers and investors, and the removal of continuing barriers to retail financial services. This would ensure more consumer choice, while at the same time cultivating consumer confidence and protection. Further concerns revolved around the need for cooperation among supervisors and an integrated EU infrastructure. Finally, it argued for the streamlining and clarification of the EU legislative apparatus and process. Discussions in the FSPG started to identify compromise between member states and put meat on the bones of the FSAP, which was launched in May 1999, with a completion date set for 2005 and securities and risk capital markets to be completed by the end of 2003.

Issues with the FSAP: macro and micro uploading and European integration

The European Council meetings at Vienna and Cardiff illustrate examples of macro uploading to the EU, with member states sharing a set of beliefs concerning efficiency, choice and effective regulation in the formulation of the SEM in financial services. This is then taken up further in the discussions undertaken at supranational, national and sub-national levels (European Commission, representatives of finance ministers and financial services interest groupings). Further interaction between En2 and European Integration was observed when the plan was endorsed at the Cologne European Council in 1999 followed by a more detailed strategy in March 2002 at the Lisbon European Council. The Lisbon Council indicated a completion date of 2005 and a number of short/medium-term priorities: these included access to investment capital and a review of the ISD, a single passport for issuers, co-operations between regulators and cross-border comparatives of financial statements. Fundamentally, the main objectives of the FSAP were provisions to ensure the extension of mutual recognition over harmonization and that supervisory institutions collaborate further in the pursuit of an efficient EU financial services market.

Initial developments for a single market in financial services took place following the implementation of the Single European Act (SEA). The SEA outlined a single market in services and capital and the governments of the day and sub-national interests were involved in the formulation of legislation to ensure the market. In this context, macro and micro uploading interactions with European integration may be observed in the formulation of EU directives. In phase two, we may observe uploading from member states at Inter Governmental Conferences (IGCs) in terms of Financial Services; a Framework for Action and the FSAP. However, again the process incorporates interaction between En2 and European integration processes. For instance, even though the IGC put the wheels in motion, the Framework for Action was developed through EU institutions holding 'extensive consultations with users, providers and supervisors of financial services' (European Commission, 1998, p. 1). Conclusions were then put to member state representation in the FSPG, and through member states and EU institutions working together, they finalized the FSAP. The main areas to be discussed by the FSPG were outlined by the Commission in the Framework for Action. One objective was to 'break the log-jam on a number of high profile proposals...which include those on take-over bids, the winding-up and liquidation of credit institutions and its sister proposal for insurance and the European Company Statute. These proposals have been held hostage for protracted periods – in some cases over a decade – by a series of political divergences' (European Commission, 1999b, pp. 2–3). Indeed, the main emphasis of the FSPG was to work with domestic actors to ensure agreement regarding these proposals 'as a token of the new political commitment to financial market modernisation' (ibid., p. 3).

Member states are able to upload macro domestic perspectives to the EU within the remit that has already been identified by the Commission within the Framework for Action which informs the FSAP and future directives. At the same time micro uploading is undertaken by sub-national interests in respect of specific legislation. The European Commission (2003, p. 1) concluded that 'progress towards adopting the necessary legislative measures and create an integrated market remains on the right track' for completion of an SEM in financial services by 2005. 'In December 2002, the Market Abuse Directive was adopted...followed by the adoption of Pension Funds Directive and amendments to the Company Law Directives' (ibid., p. 2). Furthermore, through interaction between domestic bodies and EU institutions agreement has been reached on Savings Taxation and the Prospectus Directives. Proposals were in motion regarding the Listed Company Transparency Directive. However, proposals on prospectuses, savings taxation, takeover bids and transparency of listed companies as well as revisions of the ISD still had to be adopted. Overall, although the FSAP is close to completion as 'measures come into force attention should...focus their correct and timely implementation, application and enforcement. To this end co-ordination between regulators and supervisors in the European Union should be strengthened' (European Commission, 2002, p. 2).

The European Commission identified further priorities following problems relating to companies, stock market valuation and public confidence in EU financial markets. In this context, the European Commission adopted two Communications regarding company law, corporate governance and statutory audits. Indeed, an important initiative to restore confidence in the area of corporate governance saw an interaction between sub-national, national and supranational actors when a group of company law experts was set up to deal with issues relating to company law (European Commission, 2002). In November 2002, the group presented its findings and the 'Council subsequently invited the Commission to develop, in close consultation with member states and the European Parliament an Action Plan for Company Law including corporate governance as soon as possible' (ibid., p. 2).

Legislative measures should be adopted by member states by April 2004 and a sustained effort by national, supranational and sub-national institutions in the realization of compromise regarding the remaining problems (ibid.). Further work regarding the development of FSAP was ongoing and the case for completion remained imperative; its completion would ensure the continuation of stability and integrity in EU financial markets as it paved the way for ever closer union in the area of financial services. The FSAP will also ensure that accession states will be smoothly absorbed into the EU regulatory structure (ibid.). The Internal Market Commissioner Frits Bolkestein noted that 'benefits from further integrating financial markets in the EU are huge...It will make the EU economy more competitive, efficient, innovative and thus improve prospects of the EU meeting its target of becoming the most dynamic and competitive economy in the world by 2010. The FSAP is a motor for growth' (cited in European Commission, 2002, p. 1).

Conclusion

There are elements of Europeanization and European integration processes working together in the development of a single market in financial services. Once uploaded exactitudes of the market have been developed they are downloaded to the domestic level in the form of policy and polity instruments. Rules regulations and institutions at the domestic level are influenced by EU policy. However, downloading does not mean complete uniformity. Each member state will interpret polity and policy in different ways and diversity in regulatory structures and institutional form will continue to exist.

Overall, each part of the 'process' may be broken down into 'situations', but is best understood as a 'process' because each constituent part overlaps. Consequently, full understanding necessitates comprehension of each situation in relation to the 'process' as a whole. Substantive theory provides concise explanation and can clearly identify cause and effect, whereas extending the study towards meso theory begins to provide depth of understanding through acknowledging 'process'.

Following the first phase of the SEM in financial services, member states and the EU institutions considered that the drive towards a single market in financial services had faltered. Indeed, there was further macro uploading of shared beliefs by member state governments and through this uploading and European integration processes the FSAP was formulated (in this way we observe an interaction between macro uploading and European integration procedures). On the other hand, we identify links between macro En2 and European integration theory in terms of uploading national preferences to supranational institutions.

The FSAP is made up of elements relating to macro uploading, European integration and (following involvement from the financial services sector in the form of micro uploading), further downloading. In this context, the FSAP is a means by which EU policy preferences (brought about through En2 and European integration) can be formulated into directives and downloaded to member states. This has been and is being achieved through the European Commission working with member states to implement the FSAP by creating a single EU capital market through a modernized EU legislative framework, for example, prospectus and accounting legislation, the development of open retail markets and a re-assessment of prudential supervision.

10
Europeanization Impacts on Member State Financial Services: Case Studies of the United Kingdom, Germany, Italy and Poland

Introduction

The EU environment (or political space at the EU level) encompasses European integration theory and procedures; uploading, downloading and crossloading incorporate Europeanization. On the one hand, Europeanization can be seen as the source of change in relation to the EU level in terms of European integration and the development of supranational institutions. On the other hand, European integration can be seen as the source of change and Europeanization the outcome of change on member state governmental, legal and regulatory structures. Fundamentally, we have interactions between Europeanization and European integration in the construction and perpetuation of supranational institutions and development of EU and domestic policies and systems. Europeanization incorporates uploading from the member states, which can be undertaken by government (macro En2), interest groups, sectors or companies (micro En2). At some point Europeanization becomes European integration (this is difficult to pinpoint because of the continual interaction between the two areas) this is where EU institutions develop legislation, which is eventually downloaded (En1) to member states. Indeed, change can be indicated through European regulations and directives, which, on the one hand, are directly downloaded by the EU and, on the other, downloaded through domestic legislatures. In the latter case, En1 provides the opportunity for greater interpretation and diversity throughout the EU. En3 can be observed through crossloading, which is defined as vertical policy transfer (VPT).

Through a study of financial services this chapter illustrates these intricacies (for further on this conceptualization of Europeanization and European integration see Chapter 3) and identifies downloading to three existing member states and one accession state. One member state from each of the categories outlined in Chapter 7 is reviewed in detail regarding downloaded financial services policy. The three member states from the above categories that will be dealt with in this way are the United Kingdom (liberal), Germany (prescribed) and Italy (state-controlled). Since it is the largest, Poland was selected as the accession state. The chapter builds on the structure of member state regulation identified in Chapter 8 and illustrates how the different structures have reacted to the concept of the 'competent authority' and other issues outlined in the directives.

Case Study One: downloading and the United Kingdom – the structure of the UK financial services sector

Introduction

In general, EU directives have been downloaded to the United Kingdom in the following way, the First Non-Life Insurance Directive (1973) was downloaded through the Consolidated Insurance Companies Act (1974) and the First Life Assurance Directive (1979) through the Insurance Companies Act (1982). The Second and Third generations of insurance/assurance directives were downloaded through the Insurance Companies Act (1994) and along with aspects of the Second Banking Directive (1989) through the Financial Services and Marketing Act (FSMA) (2000). However, problems still exist in terms of insurance, banking, securities and capital markets and further uploading (En2), downloading (En1) and European integration was still apparent and ongoing in the financial services sector.

As noted in Chapter 7, the United Kingdom industry was primarily liberal and supervised through the Department of Trade and Industry (DTI) with regulation revolving around solvency control, which relied on the principle of 'freedom with disclosure'. Following the Financial Services Act (1986), overall control moved to the Treasury but their involvement was limited and regulation was implemented through the Securities and Investment Board (SIB) and Self-Regulatory Organizations (SROs). There were four main SROs, which were answerable to SIB: the Securities and Futures Authority (SFA), the Investment Management Regulatory Organization (IMRO), the Life Assurance and Unit Trust Regulatory Organization (LAUTRO) and the Financial Intermediaries, Managers and Brokers Regulatory Association (FIMBRA). On top of this, some functions of banks and building societies were regulated by SROs and others by the Bank of England and the Building Societies Commission, respectively. Furthermore, Recognised Investment Exchanges (RIEs) were regulated by SIB and the Bank of England, Recognised Clearing Houses (RCHs) by SIB and professional firms by both Recognised Professional Bodies (RPBs) and SROs both of which were answerable to the SIB. In a practical context, this meant that independent advisers were regulated by the SFA, IMRO and FIMBRA; or unit trust management companies by the SFA, IMRO and LAUTRO, which caused confusion for the consumer, company and regulator. The complicated structure and limited co-operation between regulators led to issues of under-regulation in terms of mis-selling and bad advice. In 1995, there were attempts to clarify the process when LAUTRO and FIMBRA were merged into the Personal Investment Authority (PIA), however this did little to deal with the overlapping of competences regarding the supervision of the sector. The regulatory structure was supposed to ensure efficient expert regulation, however, the problem was that although these bodies were independent in name they were closely tied to the financial services sector and may have been 'captured'? Indeed, in an attempt to move away from self-regulation and the problems of capture a statutory independent authority was initiated in 1997; the Financial Services Authority (FSA).

The FSA as downloaded 'competent authority'

As outlined in the directives, as a 'competent authority', the FSA aimed to promote public understanding and maintain confidence in the financial system. This may be achieved through ensuring the right balance of consumer protection in terms of vetting entry to the market and helping to reduce financial crime. The FSA aimed to ensure these objectives in an efficient and responsible manner with a balance between the burden to the firm and the benefits to the consumer. Protection should be balanced to ensure innovation and competition between companies. This in turn will ensure competitive UK financial services in the international environment. The PIA dealt with many of these issues, but failed to deal with some fundamental problems with the industry in terms of intermediaries, commission and expertise. Indeed, through being given greater powers in terms of authorization (outlined in the directives) the FSA began dealing with these issues as well as consolidating financial services supervision. In this context, we are locating examples of downloading through En1 and diversity of interpretation in terms of fit and misfit regarding existing regulations.

In line with stipulations indicated in financial services directives the FSA attempted to ensure consumer confidence, and that only companies that displayed adequate resources and fit and proper management were authorized. The FSA also aimed to ensure fair treatment at the point of sale and clear ongoing information for consumers, for example transparent performance indicators. Overall, the FSA investigated unauthorized activities and where necessary fairness in marketing and advertising. It also dealt with mortgage endowment policies and issues of redress. These could be noted as examples of En1, however; the European Bureau of Consumers Union (EBUC) argued that there was limited access to the SEM because of diverse consumer protection rules. Consumers purchasing policies through insurance companies from other member states will not know under whose jurisdiction the contract resided and will not have adequate protection (McGee and Heusel, 1995). The membership of EBUC (member state consumer groups) micro uploaded (En2) these concerns to the EU through the pressure group and promoted the harmonization of insurance contract law.

Through En1, the FSA has recently taken on further duties. Following the Insurance Mediation Directive responsibility is being downloaded for the regulation of sales of insurance products, including home and car policies. Additional responsibilities include the regulation of mutual societies, unfair terms in financial services contracts, Lloyd's insurance market, market abuse and applications and supervision of overseas investment exchanges. This relied on the effective supervision of investment exchanges and financial services in other states or effective downloading throughout the EU. Of course, different cultural models will identify different interpretations of the directives and this leads to diversification in the EU. As noted earlier, even though uploading and European integration provide unification, the downloading procedures allow flexibility of interpretation and consequent diversity.

One may argue that national variables and globalization, rather than Europeanization, were the impetus behind the creation of the FSA as 'competent authority'. For instance, problems with the UK system had already been identified following shortcomings regarding the mis-selling of pensions, the Maxwell affair, company and banking collapses, for example Barings and Bank of Credit and Commerce International (BCCI) and endowment mortgage mis-selling. However, even though these variables existed, regulation needed to be brought in line with the rest of the EU and En1 or downloading provided a platform for uploading British preferences to the EU, for example the FSA identifying models for future EU market and supervisory structures.

During the formulation of the Third Life Assurance Directive, the UK life insurance industry was involved in successful uploading and many parts of it could have been met by the PIA and other existing British regulatory structures. However, considering the tasks necessary to supervise cross-border, and the model of an independent central bank, a single statutory supervisory institution best fitted the bill. Issues outlined in the directive would be better served by a single institution and identified an element of misfit for the UK structure (McGee and Heusel, 1995, p. 85). Even though uploading was successful, downloading necessitated institutional change. Germany also moved towards a single regulator, further evidence that the model provided the best fit for EU legislation regarding financial services in general (Germany is discussed in more detail later). However, following the adoption of a single statutory regulator the FSA has been outlining the benefits of this model throughout the EU, which illustrates some of the problems relating to policy transfer, for example do German changes to these regulatory structures incorporate vertical transfer, En3? Has Germany learned from other member states or has such a convergence been brought about through EU legislation?

Vertical or horizontal policy transfer: FSA as uploader?

Since its inception FSA representatives have argued at many EU conferences and symposia for the completion of the SEM in financial services and a specific form of regulatory structure. In some instances this may be seen as an attempt at uploading (En2) or (VPT/En3). In this way the FSA could be seen as attempting to transfer policy outcomes of downloading regarding a specific model of regulation and the future of financial services in the EU. As an outcome of En1, En2 and European integration the 'competent authority' (FSA) has become part of the process and transfers policy preferences throughout the EU or En3, which through En2 and European integration procedures become part of En1 or downloading. It is difficult to determine whether the model the FSA proposed and the means by which this is achieved incorporated En3 or En2. As an outcome of En1 the FSA could be seen as proposing EU stipulations and actions as En3. However, Britain has interpreted financial services directives and the stipulations regarding a competent authority in a specific way. Indeed, the FSA could be seen as attempting to convince other member states of the superiority of the British interpretation and consequent model and in this context its actions may encapsulate En3.

For example, Howard Davies (the head of the FSA until 2003) (2000a) argued that formal and informal barriers to cross-border trade still existed and further reforms of the SEM were necessary. He considered that to deal with the situation, two changes were paramount: (a) the legislative process needed to become more efficient; (b) the network of EU regulators needed to be strengthened and if they were to become more effective they needed greater powers. Davies (2000) also argued that regulatory structures needed to be developed in response to changing markets at the national, European and international levels. Financial markets are not confined by national boundaries, especially in the context of the EU. The EU needed to interact with the international community and be attractive to external capital and realize that regulation was not the only barrier to cross-border trade because cultural differences also existed. Primarily, Davies (2000) argued that regulatory complexity should be simplified because even though co-operation between regulators existed complexity exacerbated these relationships. Fundamentally, he thought that considering the change in the industry, regulators should work towards greater convergence.

Davies (2000a) did not propose a single regulator for securities because he thought this would be premature given the diversity regarding regulation and cultural interpretation in separate member states. He thought that 'without harmonized regulation, or the ability to enforce its regulations, a pan-European securities regulator would be ineffective' (ibid., p. 3). This does suggest that if regulations were harmonized, and a pan-European regulator able to enforce these regulations, then such an institution would be effective. However, there would also be accountability problems concerning the European Parliament, European Commission and member state governments.

Furthermore, Davies (2000a) thought similar arguments applied to banking, and that as with most sectors in the EU, supervision should be enforced through regulatory networks under a common legislative framework. For instance, the Brouwer Report considered that EU banking supervision was adequate and would remain so, as long as regulatory networks were enhanced (cited in Davies, 2000, 2000a). These are further examples of the FSA not only reflecting elements of a downloaded institution but because of a concern for the regulatory structure emerging in the EU it transfers its own perception of acceptable future institutions based on downloaded interpretations of policy and developments (VTP/En3). In part, the FSA is an example of downloading from the EU (this will be analysed in more detail in the following section of this chapter).

Of course, (as identified by other member states) it did not need to take this form but the agreed structure did allow it to deal with stipulations outlined by directives in an efficient and effective manner. If cross-border trade in financial services was to be realized through home country control, member states were obliged to ensure clear lines of demarcation when it came to regulatory structures and the FSA provided this in the United Kingdom. However, the FSA also provided an example of policy transfer whereby it was involved in discussions regarding inputs to EU legislation and activities relating to European integration (which could border on uploading).

En2 or En3: FSA as uploader?

As noted above, since its inception FSA representatives have argued at many EU conferences and symposia for the completion of the SEM in financial services and a specific form of regulatory structure. In some instances this may be seen as an attempt at uploading (En2) or crossloading (En3). In this way the FSA could be seen as trying to crossload outcomes of downloading regarding a specific model of regulation and the future of financial services in the EU. As an outcome of En1, En2 and European integration the downloaded structure or FSA has become part of the 'process' and transfers policy preferences throughout the EU (this could be seen as uploading but this may involve 'conceptual stretching'), which through European integration procedures become part of En1 or downloading.

It is difficult to determine whether the model the FSA champions and the means by which this is achieved incorporates En3 or micro En2. As an outcome of En1 the FSA could be seen as proposing EU stipulations and actions as En3. The United Kingdom has interpreted financial services directives and the stipulations regarding a 'competent authority' in a specific way. Indeed, the FSA could be seen as attempting to convince other member states of the superiority of the British interpretation and consequent model and in this context its actions could encapsulate vertical policy transfer.

Conclusions

There are examples of crossloading, uploading and downloading as well as European integration process and theory in the formulation of directives and the regulatory structure in financial services. However, when these separate parts of the 'process' are identified it is difficult to break them down as each 'situation' overlaps the other. Furthermore, 'content' in the form of shared beliefs can also be observed. This may be seen clearly when we look at the Third Life Assurance Directive, 'competent authorities', the FSA and the FSAP. The FSAP indicated that an SEM in financial services had been under construction since 1973. Following the shared belief between member states that an SEM was necessary, domestic and European interest groups uploaded preferences to EU policy-making institutions, which through European integration processes formulated legislation that was then downloaded to member states.

This may be seen clearly through the idea of a 'competent authority' that has been downloaded through the directives. The United Kingdom adopted the single regulator model of the FSA, which has since developed its role and begun to take an active part in En3 throughout the EU. This has involved some interaction with European integration. However, it remains to be seen whether the FSA will become a full time active uploader.

Overall, each part of the 'process' may be broken down into 'situations', but is best understood as a 'process' because each constituent part overlaps, so full understanding necessitates comprehension of each 'situation' in relation to the 'process' as a whole. The FSA is made up of elements relating to macro uploading, European integration and (following involvement from the financial services sector in the form of micro uploading) downloading and crossloading.

Case Study Two: German downloading and crossloading

Introduction

As outlined in Chapter 7, the German regulatory structure was prescribed and even though the industry called for this structure to be relaxed, it was strongly felt that some levels of regulation were necessary. In terms of the development of a 'competent authority' the German system displayed elements identified in the directives. There was a preponderance of liberalization in the German system, however, Hans Eichel the German Finance Minister in 2003 considered that in liberalizing its markets Germany also realized the necessity for strong regulation to ensure fair play. Initially there was minimal change to the German structure, however, in 2002 a major overhaul was completed.

The new regulator was similar to the FSA and took over supervision of banking, insurance and security markets. The Federal Financial Supervisory Authority (BaFIN) was established in April 2002. In May 2002, it took over the former functions of the supervisory authorities for banking (BAKred), securities (BAWe) and insurance (BAV). Consequently BaFIN is now the single regulator for German financial services in terms of solvency, supervision and consumer protection. The reasons for this change are uncertain as they indicate some of the difficulties in distinguishing between En3, En2 and En1. This Case Study deals with these difficulties as it attempts to ascertain the problems faced by Germany in dealing with downloaded policy. Furthermore, the chapter analyses the German Banking Act (1998) and illustrates aspects of downloading and European integration in the formulation of this legislation.

Rationales for a single competent authority: downloading or vertical policy transfer?

There were a number of reasons for the formation of a single regulator in terms of the integration of financial products and cross-sectoral strategies. This is illustrated in other member states, which over the last few years have 'established modern integrated supervisory structures' (BaFIN, 2002, p. 2). BaFIN was instituted to provide effective comprehensive supervision and avoid competitive imbalances that a fragmented regulatory structure could precipitate. Because the regulator is responsible for all market participants it falls into the category of the 'competent authority' outlined by recent financial services directives. BaFIN simplified the German regulatory structure which meant that it limited the number of supervisory offices external member state companies needed to deal with when entering the market and more importantly, it facilitated information between other member state regulators and kept contact with other member state companies to a minimum. Furthermore, a unified regulator not only offered an explicit point of contact for other member state regulators it also provided distinct representation at the European and international levels. The new German regulator would carry more weight in international supervisory forums and as a result German interests could be represented more effectively at an international level. In relation to the EU this may take the form of micro En2 or En3.

In terms of En1 the Banking Act (1998) amendments outlined the role for BaFIN when it stated that 'when supervising institutions which conduct banking business or provide financial services in another state of the European Economic Area and when supervising institutions as provided in the Banking Directive, the Federal financial Supervisory Authority...shall co-operate with the competent authorities of the state concerned' (ibid., Division 2, Section 8, Para. 3). If BaFIN omitted a company from undertaking business in Germany, it would need to inform the 'competent authorities' of other states where the company had business and identify the measures it was intending to take to terminate these infringements (ibid., Section 8, Para. 4). Furthermore, BaFIN may not supervise a group if it is

> domiciled in another state of the European Economic Area, in that other state, is included in supervision on a consolidated basis in accordance with the Banking Directive, or in the case of financial holdings these groups are supervised on a consolidated basis in accordance with the Banking Directives by the 'competent authorities' of another state of the European Economic Area. A precondition of such exemption is an agreement of the Federal

Financial Supervisory Authority with the competent authorities of the other state. The Commission of the European Communities is to be informed of the existence and contents of such agreements. (ibid., Section 8a)

The Banking Act also outlines financial obligations of institutions in terms of 'assets entrusted to them' and 'adequate own funds'. In accordance with legislation indicated by the EU relating to these areas the 'Federal Ministry of Finance shall draw up solvency principles by which the Federal Financial Supervisory Authority will, in normal cases, assess whether the requirements ... have been satisfied' (ibid., Part 2, Division 1, Section 10, Para. 1). Fundamentally, approval of a company must be compatible with 'the framework laid down by European Community legislation' (ibid., Para. 1b).

In this way we can observe downloading from the EU through the Banking Act (1998). The Act initially dealt with many of the issues outlined in financial service directives and further amendments have dealt with arising issues from new EU directives. For instance the amendment regarding insolvency and banking law, of Article 3 in December 1999, specifically dealt with the directive on settlement finality in payment and securities settlement systems (Directive 98/26/EC, see OJ No L 166, p. 45). Further amendments have dealt with legislation relating to 'competent authorities' as noted above amendment April 2002 and financial obligations.

Even though there are similarities regarding BaFIN and other member state regulatory authorities it is still based on its own historical circumstance and interpretations of EU directives best suited to the German financial services sector. BaFIN is made up of three directorates each based on previously independent regulators and three departments, which deal with cross-sectoral issues. The first directorate deals with banking supervision based on the German Banking Act, Mortgage Bank Act and Building Society Act. Each of these took into consideration EU stipulations. For example as well as capital adequacy provisions and compliance with statutory risk limits, a company must ensure professionally qualified reliable management. Indeed, these are stipulations found in the remits of other member state regulators especially those of the FSA. The second directorate deals with insurance supervision based on Insurance Supervision Law (VAG). The main objectives are to ensure that liabilities are met and the insured protected. The third directorate supervises securities and asset management. In addition to the direcorates there are three cross-sectoral departments: the first has responsibility for financial markets and international issues, the second consumer protection and the third, money laundering. BaFIN's first cross-sectoral department also co-ordinated the institutions involvement with European and international organization; 'BaFIN is represented in many international forums (and) participates in the elaboration of homogeneous regulatory standards within the EU' (BaFIN, 2002, p. 6). As with the FSA this starts to question the role of BaFIN at the EU level. Indeed, there were indications that it was involved in En2 but there was limited evidence at this stage regarding En3.

Insurance Supervision Law (2002 Amendment) provided the basis for freedom of services in Germany. 'Insurance undertakings which have their head office in another member state of the European Community or another signatory state of the EEA agreement (home member state) may ... carry on direct insurance business in Germany via a branch or under the freedom of services provision' (Section 110a, Para. 1). If a company wished to undertake business through a branch, home member state supervisors should furnish the documentation identified in the third generation of insurance directives regarding ability to trade. This is where an undertaking that decides to trade in another member state should advise their 'competent authority' of this intention. Furthermore, the member state required undertakings that proposed to establish a branch to identify a scheme of the types of business envisaged, provide an address for correspondence and name the branch's authorized agent (92/96/EEC, Art. 10, Section 2, Paras a–d). Business conducted under freedom of services cannot be undertaken until the company informs the home supervisor of its intention and the home 'competent authority' informs BaFIN (within one month) of the solvency margins, classes of insurance that the company has authorization to offer and the nature of commitments to be covered in the host member state (ibid., Arts 11, 14 and 17). 'Financial supervision of any such business activities is the sole responsibility of the supervisory authority of the home member state' (Insurance Supervision Law 2002 Amendment; Section 110a, Para. 3). However, with regard to health insurance BaFIN continually informs the 'competent authorities' of other member states about legal provisions host companies should follow if it wishes to carry out business in Germany. In this context, we observe the means by which the 'general good' may be brought into operation. If BaFIN considers that a company is not conforming with regulations on health insurance it can inform the home 'competent authority' of measures it may take regarding this and request its co-operation. If both this and other punitary measures are unsuccessful then BaFIN can prohibit the 'undertaking from continuing to do business in Germany wholly or partly' (ibid., Section 111b, Para. 1). In the main, these stipulations are reciprocal and BaFIN provides the services outlined in both the Banking Act and Insurance Supervising Law in relation to German companies undertaking business in other member states.

Conclusion

Caio Koch-Weiser (2002) indicated that strategies to ensure a European financial market in the short to medium term (2005) needed to be developed at the national and supranational levels. He argued that the German financial services market needed to improve and that a more liberal German stock exchange would be more competitive at the international level. Based on the FSAP the German strategy aimed to ensure a number of objectives, which include harnessing institutional expertise in the policy-making process, horizontally integrating insurance, banking and financial markets, considering the role of Deutschbank and the implications of the EU. Fundamentally, the German programme reflected that of the EU because a unified strategy and outcome would provide a greater voice for the EU at IMF and World Bank meetings and ensure a competitive but appropriately regulated international financial market. Germany is heavily involved in uploading and European integration processes. Furthermore, as can be observed through the Banking Act and insurance Supervision law it closely adheres to EU legislation as it downloads EU directives regarding the financial services sector.

Case Study Three: downloading and diversity in Italy

Introduction

In Chapter 7, the Italian financial services sector was identified as having a state-controlled regulatory structure. This has changed dramatically over the last ten years with the Italian sector now privatized and a clearer regulatory structure in place 'Italy is changing. The deep influence of European integration is the major agent of change. On the one side, the European model – whatever this means – has inspired and introduced reforms. On the other, the factual and cognitive constraints set by the EU have favoured – if not indirectly compelled – many of these transformations' (Mario Monti, 1998, p. 13, cited in Giulani, 2001, p. 48).

With regard to the changes taking place in Italy as with other member states it is sometimes, if not always, difficult to determine cause and effect. Giulani (2001) argued that since the 1990s, Europeanization has been considered as normalization in Italy. This may take the form of the 'idealization of foreign experiences' and the 'role of Italy on the international scene' (p. 51). Indeed, changes in Italy may be considered as driven by domestic, European or global variables. 'The Europeanization of Italy certainly goes through this wider process of gaining international credibility' (p. 52). However, Giulani goes on to consider that Europeanization in Italy is clearly discernable in terms of public consciousness, policy networks and discourse that defines and determines ideas and policy-making in a number of sectors (ibid.).

'In many ways Italy today is a new Italy' (Prodi, 1999, p. 49, cited in Giulani, 2001, p. 47). This change has taken many forms however, this Case Study deals with changes in relation to privatization and liberalization in terms of financial services, examines the regulatory structure following these changes and identifies the extent they may be outcomes of En1, European integration and En3.

En1 and Italian financial services regulation

In 1993, *Testerio Unico Bancario* (TUB) reorganized the Italian regulatory structure and dealt with issues identified in the EU's first and second banking directives in terms of prudent management, stability regarding banks and the system, efficiency, competitiveness and compliance. However, financial services regulation was revisited later in the decade and now comes mainly under Legislative Decree No. 58 1998 *Testo Unico della Finanza* or the Consolidated Law on Financial Intermediation (CLFI). This clarified the division of labour regarding supervisory responsibility between the Italian central bank and the securities regulator (CONSOB).

It [CLFI] provides comprehensive regulation of securities intermediaries, financial markets and central depositaries of financial
instruments and issuers. The provisions governing intermediaries
confirm the principle of assigning supervisory responsibilities to
objective, entrusting the Bank of Italy with safeguarding financial
stability and CONSOB with ensuring transparent and proper conduct. The bank of Italy is also charged with defining the prudential rules for limiting risk that investment undertakings must
follow. (Bank of Italy, 1999, p. 171)

Financial stability regulation was the objective of the Bank of Italy and
transparency and business conduct regulation the tasks of CONSOB.
The CLFI builds on TUB and further reorganized the Italian regulatory
structure and completed the privatization process. Overall, the CLFM
provided a clear example of En1, as a policy mechanism that modernized and reorganized 'Italian legislation governing securities intermediaries, financial markets and issuers' (Bank of Italy, 1999, p. 204).

The CLFI identified that banking regulation in Italy was to be
administered through the Bank of Italy, the Treasury and the Comitato
Interministeriale per il Credito ed il Risparmio (CICR). These institutions regulated banking groups and financial intermediaries ensuring
capital adequacy, risk limitation, accounting procedures permissible
holdings and company control mechanisms. In the other member
states discussed in this text, monetary policy and supervision of the
financial services sector are separate, however, in Italy supervision of
banks is the responsibility of the Bank of Italy. As noted earlier, the
securities market is regulated by CONSOB, which aimed to ensure consumer protection in terms of accurate and transparent information in
relation to market participants and prospectuses. These are issues identified in the ISD and under discussion between the domestic and
European levels as member states and the EU attempt to develop
European investment markets in line with FSAP deadlines.

An earlier legislative decree No. 576, 1982 instituted the insurance
and reinsurance regulator Instituto per la Vigilanzasull Assicurazioni
Private de Interesse Collectivo (ISVAP). As noted in Chapter 7 ISVAP
actions were authorized through government guidelines and dealt
with technical, financial and competency of management issues.
Legislative decrees No. 174–5 in 1995 implemented the second and
third generation of life and non-life insurance directives. Overall,

legislation has attempted to bring the Italian financial services market and regulatory structure further into line with other member states and in this context may be interpreted as En1 or En3. However, the Italian market and financial services structure is still different to other member states in terms of continuity and consistency, with separate regulatory institutions or 'competent authorities'.

ISVAP has supervisory powers regarding consumer protection, solvency margins, technical provisions and adequate assets in the context of covering these margins and provisions. As well as ensuring the solvency and efficiency of undertakings ISVAP is responsible for ensuring the stability of the insurance market and is able to grant companies authorization to trade in insurance or extend into other areas of insurance business. Indeed, in providing authorization, it verified that trading requirements were met not only for Italy, but the EU in general. As noted earlier, in 1995 a clear example of En1 was identified when legislation was enacted that implemented the second and third generation of insurance directives. This meant that ISVAP extended its remit and supervised companies with head offices in Italy, as well as business that these companies may undertake in the rest of the EU. Furthermore, through the EU and links with other member state 'competent authorities' greater collaboration between domestic institutions became necessary. This was made easier through clear demarcations regarding responsibility between separate regulators, which in the United Kingdom may have caused confusion. It remains to be seen whether the Italians adhere to their model when the general trend does seem to be towards single regulators and demarcations between monetary policy and banking supervision.

The CLFM provided a legal framework to ensure that Italian security intermediaries could compete in the SEM. 'The consolidated law confirms the innovations introduced in 1996 with the incorporation in Italian legislation of EEC Directive 93/22 of 10 May 1993 on investment services in the securities field' (Bank of Italy, 1999, p. 204). The CLFM also had implications for the market structure through completing changes made under Legislative Decree 415, 1996 and transposing the ISD and CAD Directives, which ended the security markets status as public institutions. Indeed, security markets were privatized as the Italian market structure moved away from state-controlled regulatory structures that were outlined in Chapter 7 towards a more prescribed/liberal structure.

Security markets became 'entities established under private law and endowed with self regulation powers, although they are still subject to control by the supervisory authorities' (ibid., p. 205). The CLMF implemented EC directive 95/26/EC (which following the BCCI affair) in terms of accounts related tasks and EEC Directive 91/308 in terms of money laundering. Furthermore, secondary legislation downloaded both EU and international (Basel Accord) and EU stipulations (95/26/EC) regarding compulsory reserves laid down by the ECB and Regulation of December 1998, in relation to the former and internal controls and compulsory reserves in terms of the latter. Legislative Decree 333 of August 1999 completed the downloading of 95/26/EC, which had initially been transposed through the CLMF. In this context, both Europeanization and global variables may be detected however, in the main we can observe major aspects of En1 in Italian financial services.

Further downloaded EU directives involved cross-border credit transfers, 97/5/EC in 2000 and 2001; Electronic money institutions, 2000/28/EC and 2000/46/EC in 2002; winding-up of credit institutions 2001/24/EC in 2003; financial collateral arrangements, 2002/47/EC in 2003; and investment funds and open-end investment companies, 2001/107/EC and 2001/108/EC in 2003. The process has speeded up since the FSAP and numerous pieces of secondary legislation dealt with problem areas of legislation and further emphasized Europeanization and European integration.

There is an interaction between the global, EU and domestic levels of policy-making. For instance in 1999 the Basel Committee proposed a new capital adequacy framework for the banking sector. 'In close co-ordination with the work of the Basel Committee the European Union launched an initiative to revise the Community directives on capital adequacy' (Bank of Italy, 2000, p. 183). This was intensified in early 2001 when the EU began a second period of consultation regarding the reform of capital requirements. The consultation document declared that the EU legislative framework should incorporate stipulations laid down in the new Basel accord and that these should be included in the FSAP. Moreover, in 2003, the Basel Committee released a third consultation document, which simplified previous proposals. 'The Committee ... decided to ask banks to carry out stress tests on their levels of capital adequacy. The exercise will allow the supervisory authorities to check that intermediaries have sufficient capital buffers to absorb the effects of the business cycle, thereby avoiding credit supply restrictions' (Bank of Italy, 2003, p. 206). This process illustrated interaction between the levels of policy-making and identified differences between En1, European integration and En2.

Conclusions

Overall, the Italian regulatory structure deals with EU financial services directives in terms of market structure and supervision. On the one hand, EU directives are now downloaded quite quickly and in the main adhere quite closely to stipulations identified in the legislation. On the other hand, the Italian interpretation of the 'competent authority' outlined in the directives indicates that issues can be dealt with in terms of diversity; that even though EU policy is aimed at integration the very nature of the process allows room for cultural diversity.

The Italian regulatory structure also indicated problems when identifying cause and effect or dependent and independent variables when it comes to European integration, Europeanization and Globalization. Indeed, the interactions between the Basel Committee, the EU and member states in terms of capital adequacy make this very clear. In certain instances, it is difficult to determine the rationale behind the regulatory reforms. However, other areas of financial service regulation provided clear examples of En1, European integration, En3 and En2 even if the difference between them was sometimes a little opaque. As noted by the Governor of the Bank of Italy following the shareholder meeting in 2003, 'We are strongly committed to playing our part in the formulation of the Eurosystem policy and its implementation at the national level' (Bank of Italy, 2003, p. 1).

Case Study Four: Poland and Europeanization – a case of downloading

Introduction

As a non-member of the EU, over the past 12 years Poland has been preparing for membership. Following many years, under the control of the USSR, Poland had a state-controlled market structure and financial services were almost obsolete. Over the last ten years, Poland had mainly been involved in downloading aspects of Europeanization because avenues for uploading when outside of the

EU are scarce and in most instances non-existent. It is very difficult if not impossible to upload policy preference when the mechanisms are not available.

In the early 1990s, the Polish government and Polish interests saw their future in the EU and undertook strategies to achieve membership. 'For us, Poles at the time of signing the European Agreement in 1991, that joining the European communities was our supreme goal' (Cimoszewicz, 2002, p. 1). This conviction was outlined in the preamble to the agreement, which was acted on in 1994 when Poland submitted its official application. 'Poland … began striving for membership of the European Communities in the early nineties … we have behind us more than ten years of adaptations of our economies and administrations, and of preparation of our citizens for European standards' (Cimoszewicz, 2002a, p. 1). Poland saw itself as a central entity in the creation of the EU and accepted change that would ensure membership in 2004. Over the last decade, Poland has accepted downloaded EU policy even though it has not been involved in uploading or European integration procedures. However, over the next few years this will change and Poland will take its place in the policy-making process and become an uploader and active participant in European integration. This Case Study illustrates how Poland has been dealing with downloading and illustrates the changes it will encounter once it becomes active in uploading. Indeed, this Case Study identifies Hegelian 'recognition' and 'civil constitution' as Poland takes on legislation so as to fit in with existing and developing EU policy. It also identifies neo-functional issues such as spillover and supranational decisions impacting on domestic policy even though Poland is external to negotiations. However, it also exemplifies intergovernmental national preference in that this is the policy Poland has chosen to follow.

Uploading, downloading and European integration: developments in Poland

As noted earlier, since the early 1990s, Poland has downloaded EU policy to the domestic level even though it has not been involved in uploading or European integration. Through Enlargement Poland will be directly connected with the EU and involved in 'voting coalitions' in initiating and implementing EU policy. Komorowski (2003) considered that this would 'constitute a new dimension in the political culture of my country. Poland will have to learn how to co-operate within an intergovernmental institution such as the council of the EU and a supranational one – such as the European Commission' (p. 1). Indeed, Poland would be directly involved in En2 through uploading interests to EU institutions.

In many instances, in its transition from a collectivist to market economy, Poland closely reflected the changing legislation and regulatory structures that were evolving in the EU. In other words, Poland was downloading EU policy and polity even though they were not involved in either uploading or the European integration process. 'For the first time in modern history, Poland is free to express her views and take decisions as a state. Joining the EU will enable us to do the same but on the European level, together with our European partners' (Komorowski, 2003, p. 1). In fact, given that Poland had been downloading and crossloading EU policy as a non-member state, membership would involve it in both uploading and European integration and consequently extend the expression of her views. When introducing 'draft laws' the Polish government had for a number of years taken into consideration whether they were compatible with existing EU legislation (ibid.). The Polish governments had already put in place the foundations of the legal and institutional arrangements that membership would require to ensure a smooth transition into the single market and European Monetary Union (EMU). 'We are already well advanced in adjusting Polish legislation to the *acquis*. In the years 2000–01 the Polish government adopted the drafts of 142 adjustment bills, of which parliament adopted 136. The high momentum of adjustment work was evident last year in such fields as the environment, free movement of goods, fisheries, competition policy and justice – that is the areas crucial for efficient operation in the Union' (Cimoszewicz, 2002a, p. 2).

In late 2002, changes to Polish strategies started to occur in respect of EU membership. In November 2001, the Polish government outlined its strategy which indicated that membership of the EU by 2004 was a priority and identified how Poland may immediately function in the EU as an effective member state. This strategy accelerated Polish policies pursued over the previous ten years in terms of developing legislation and ensuring the broadest base agreement for accession. The success of ensuring broad based support was substantiated in June 2003 when on the basis of a 60 per cent turn-out,

78 per cent of Polish voters agreed to accession in 2004. The strategy also identified how the Polish government would progressively involve itself in macro uploading and 'play a significant role in creating a vision of a united Europe ... [and] be actively involved in the future of European integration' (Cimoszewicz, 2002a, p. 2). As accession became imminent Poland's role in terms of macro uploading became more evident. Governmental representatives began to involve themselves 'in shaping a vision of the future Europe, through active involvement in preparations for the intergovernmental conference on the new institutional shape of the European Union' (ibid., p. 3). Indeed, following agreement on accession in 2003, the polish government and Spain vehemently opposed a deal, which gave the four larger member states greater voting powers in the reformed Council of Ministers.

Poland is prepared for comprehensive integration with the EU in terms of EMU, defence and foreign policy. 'Poland's international undertakings are fully compatible with the foreign policy of the European Union' (Cimoszewicz, 2002, p. 2). The Polish authorities bought into the idea of a united Europe because of the ideals that underpin European integration, such as perpetual peace, recognition and economic regeneration. Recognition is important because if security and prosperity are to be realized then it is 'essential to build mutual trust and in accordance with one of the fundamental principles of the Union – the principle of solidarity – the "strong" must support the "weak" ... We also endorse other fundamental principles of European integration – the principles of equality and subsidiarity' (ibid.). Integration in the EU has been successful because of the active involvement and equal participation of member states and sub-national interests.

For Poland EU membership has always involved complete and full integration. For example accession to the EU has always been directly connected with membership of the EMU. As soon as the criteria for membership are met Poland intends to join the EMU. Monetary and fiscal policies to enable membership of EMU have been pursued for many years as it was envisaged that Poland would become a member of EMU by 2006/07. 'Poland will become a member of the Eurozone where transaction costs and exchange rate uncertainty relating to trade are reduced, where there is increased competition, which will hopefully deliver efficiency, productivity and reduced prices' (ibid.,

p. 2). Since the early 1990s, Poland has been on the 'difficult road of transformations and preparation for membership in the European Communities' (Cimoszewicz, 2002, p. 1). Poland now met both the political and economic criteria that membership required; it had democratic and open institutions as well as economic growth of over 36 per cent over the last ten years and direct foreign investment of USD50b, 30b of which is from the EU. Exports to the EU grew from 5b USD in 1989 to 24b in 2000 and exports from 5b to 34b (ibid.).

Bolkestein (2003) concluded that in economic terms Poland had drawn much closer to the EU over the last decade. For instance, the EU is now Poland's most important trading partner and accession will provide great benefits for both parties. However, many changes had not yet been realized and much still needed to be achieved. It was unlikely that all will be working perfectly by 2004 because even if there were clear alignment of legislation, effective enforcement would still be problematic. Free cross-border trade is still hindered in some areas through technical and administrative Non-Tariff Barriers (NTBs) and 'a stable financial services system subject to...prudential supervision...will be indispensable if Polish...banks...are to be allowed to offer their services throughout the European Union' (Bolkestein, 2003, p. 1).

Progress had been made but further work was necessary. For example, guarantees regarding the division between political interference and the financial services regulator needed to be implemented and adhered too. This is linked to the European Commission's continual moves towards institutional re-structuring and a truly open market in services, of which financial services is an integral part.

Randzio-Plath (2001) pointed out that accession states can only be full members of the EU if they implement not just 'community legislation...but also build up the institutions (public administration, competition and financial supervisory authorities, courts of justice) in order to ensure its effective application' (p. 2). He made the point that if/when accession states join the Eurozone an area of vital importance will be a sound and efficient financial services market. Poland as with the other accession countries started from scratch and the 'European Commission, national central banks and the private financial sector have been giving technical expertise and financial support in order to help accession countries in building up their financial services infrastructure' (ibid., p. 5). To deal with risks that a fragile financial sector would impose on the Single European Market (SEM) along with existing member states through En2 and especially for Poland En3 shared beliefs had developed regarding the structure of an ideal financial services sector. For example, in 1998, the Polish Securities and Exchange Commission (PSEC) ran a seminar devoted to EU directives and regulations regarding prospectus and disclosure requirements. This is important because in partnership with the Ministry of Finance the PSEC prepares documentation regarding Poland's membership of the EU in financial services and capital markets. Indeed, one of the main tasks of the PSEC was to pave the way for downloading through comparing *acquis communotaire* between national and EU legislation relating to capital markets.

Conclusion

In Poland, significant progress had been made regarding the implementation of financial services regulation. However, legislation in this area was continually in a state of flux, especially following the initiation of the FSAP. Over the past ten years, Poland has implemented far-reaching reforms in terms of the privatization of the banking sector, high-quality corporate governance, liquid capital markets, a liberalized, competitive well-regulated financial services sector, which undertakes cross-border trade in insurance, securities investment, fund management etc. Poland's 'rapid and sustained economic recovery from the initial economic recession are the reward they have reaped from effective economic management. This should stand them in good stead as they look forward to rapid integration in the European Union, its common currency and its common goods, services and capital markets' (Linn, 2001, p. 3). Poland has downloaded EU policy over the last decade to become recognized as a partner. The Polish people recognized the basis of the EU in terms of economic regeneration and prosperity and continued peaceful co-operation throughout the EU. However, have the polish people given up the opportunity to develop a regulatory structure based around their own cultural and historical perspectives? Or had cultural diversity been built into the new regulatory structure, which will become more apparent once assimilation with the SEM is complete?

11
General Conclusions

Introduction

This study attempted to deal with a number of different, disparate and complimentary issues as it investigated theoretical frameworks and methodological approaches as means of enabling greater understanding and explanation of social sciences in general and political science and European integration in particular. This work attempted to mix paradigms of inquiry and through an empirical study of insurance and broader financial services provided an understanding of European integration and Europeanization. Indeed, through the same empirical study the analysis identified levels of theory and how they may best explain the European Union (EU). Overall, the work illustrated the interactive nature of theory and practice in providing understanding and explanation of political phenomenon.

Differentiations between paradigms of inquiry identified an initial problem relating to mixing a positivist ontological perspective with the other three (post-positivist, critical theory and constructivist paradigms). This study dealt with this problem by recognizing that in the social sciences pure positivist expectations were unrealistic. Consequently, the work concentrated on post-positivism, critical theory and constructivism. Eventually, this work identified two major paradigms in positivism (mainly made up of post-positivist perspectives) and constructivism (which included the idea of a general critical theory). Given these paradigms of inquiry, the text arrived at distinctions in theoretical perspectives, and differences in the way theory can be used in explaining and/or understanding phenomenon. The work provided different levels of theory, on the one hand, and different intensities of normative expectation, on the other. For instance, the political philosophy of Kant and Hegel (which provide un-verifiable abstractions) as well as the grand theories in terms of functionalism, realism, intergovernmentalism and neo-functionalism display explicit normative perspectives even though these encompass differing degrees. Meso theories or middle-range theories such as multilevel governance, state-centricism and Europeanization express more limited normativism. Finally, substantive theories or the specifics of Europeanization En1, En2 and En3, even though as isolated variables attempt to negate normativism, as with most social science this is extremely difficult and axiological perspectives persist. In this context, this study identified the distinction between positivism and normativism and the role of theory in attempting explanation and understanding of phenomenon.

For positivism, theory is the pursuit of laws in idealized situations and explanation of phenomenon through thin data. For constructivism theory is about providing frameworks for understanding of situations and phenomenon through thick data. However, as this work has attempted to exemplify, this does not mean that the two approaches cannot be synthesized in social science studies. Through breaking down meso theory and drawing on grand theory and political philosophy the text has identified how different elements of substantive theory may be used to:

(a) Explain in positivist terms by simplifying theory and data;
(b) Synthesize elements of Europeanization and 'content' and involve elements of positivism and constructivism;
(c) Ignore positivist perspectives, and in a constructivist context build a framework for understanding phenomenon.

This meant analysing Europeanization in terms of downloading, uploading and crossloading and identifying distinctions in relation to European integration through synthesising methodological approaches.

Conceptualizing Europeanization

As noted, one major difficulty in the study was the identification of difference between Europeanization and European integration.

This analysis has attempted to overcome a number of problems relating to conceptualizations of Europeanization and the difference between Europeanization and European integration.

Europeanization can be understood from an En1, En2 or an En3 perspective. European integration is identified as the environment on which Europeanization impacts or from which it emanates. However, it is more complicated than this, with interaction between the two areas merging into one another for different lengths of time and with differing levels of intensity. This means that at different times the emphasis on Europeanization will either be based around mechanisms of change in terms of uploading from the domestic to the EU level, or downloading from the EU to the domestic level. The success of the member state in terms of uploading will have implications when it comes to downloading in respect of impacts and change on the domestic environment. The success in uploading will affect misfit and consequently have an impact on downloading in the context of fit. One may argue that this is why in most instances En1, En2 and En3 need to be brought into the equation.

Europeanization fulfils the objectives of the founding fathers of the EU in that through an interaction with European integration, domestic policies have been incrementally transformed. European integration and mechanisms of Europeanization in terms of downloading, and changes in lobbying procedures and policy-making institutions that harmonize domestic policies ensures the development of the evolving EU. Indeed, there is a spillover effect among different actors and parts of sector and polity domains in the formulation of the EU and through further uploading and European integration unity is gradually achieved, however, paradoxically diversity is always apparent.

Neo-functionalism and intergovernmentalism were considered grand theories that encompassed a range of categories themselves. One may argue that there is no single theory of intergovernmental policy-making. That it may be interpreted as an approximation of state-centric approaches to European policy-making where national government actors aim to exercise as much political control as possible in terms of competence allocation, treaty changes and policy implementation. Furthermore, the same may be said of neo-functionalism; rather than a linear theory of dynamic shifts towards a supranational body it may be understood as a touchstone for measuring theoretical departures or arrivals. Thus, it provided for substantive elements of Europeanization in the form of: sub-national interests (micro En2), functional spillover (En1 and En3), institutional spillover (macro En2, micro En2 and European integration), supranational institutions and cultivated spillover (macro En2 and European integration) intergovernmental national preferences (macro En2, European integration and En1).

The distinction between Europeanization and European integration provided further explanation regarding the transformation of European political space and identified interactions between different levels of governance. Through the actions of sub-national interests and their interactions with supranational institutions and spillover in institutional, functional and cultivated forms our theoretical framework for understanding European policy-making has been enhanced. Europeanization and multilevel governance combine elements of intergovernmentalism and neo-functionalism and this increases explanatory power, which further develops our understanding of European integration and the EU.

Empirical study: EU, SEM and financial services

Through an empirical study of the EU in general, and financial services in particular, the text has provided examples of the different ways theoretical frameworks maybe used to explain and understand phenomenon. The initial stages of the EU in terms of the European Economic Community (EEC), European Coal and Steel Community (ECSC), Euratom, European Defence Community (EDC) and European Political Community (EPC) can be understood as attempts to reinforce peaceful reconciliation and economic regeneration. In this context, they may be observed as attempts to achieve 'civil constitution' through 'recognition' and display functional and neo-functional values. Later stages bring in realist and intergovernmental variables. However, none of these indicated a positivist perspective of theory that could clearly display cause and effect; this was meant to be the role of meso and substantive theory. Through a study of financial services this analysis has attempted to illustrate the difficulties in identifying cause and effect without simplification.

In general, this study has argued that there is a deconstruction of grand European integration theories at the meso level in the form of

Europeanization and multilevel governance. This deconstruction is further realized through the breakdown of the meso theory into substantive theories – which again illuminate specific elements of the grand theories. Through an empirical study of financial services, insurance interest groups and EU policy-making institutions this study has begun to make some generalizations regarding Europeanization and European integration theory in terms of spillover, supranationality, sub-national interests and member state preferences.

In the context of methodological approaches and financial services, En1, En2 and En3, as well as European integration are involved in the formulation of directives and the market place. To attain a positivist explanation the study needs to concentrate on En1, En2 or En3 individually. This simplifies the process with En1 providing the clearest example of cause and effect. However, when these different parts of the process are identified it is difficult to break them down as each overlaps with the other, this may be seen clearly when we look at financial services directives, 'competent authorities' and the FSA. The FSAP indicated that an SEM in financial services had been under construction since 1973. This is a good example of 'process' at work and the ongoing interaction between En1, En2, En3 and European integration. The FSAP encapsulates European integration in that it builds on previous attempts to provide an SEM and incorporates utilization of uploading in the creation of rules and regulations for downloading. In this context, we can observe the formulation of directives (through uploading and European integration) in banking, insurance and capital markets. These directives and regulations are then downloaded to member states where different interpretations of policies are implemented. Unification does take place but as noted earlier there is room for cultural diversity.

In terms of the 'competent authority' outlined in the directives, the United Kingdom adopted the single regulator model or the FSA. This has since developed its role and began to take an active part in crossloading and uploading to the EU and consequently interacting with European integration. Europeanization is made up of En1, En2 and En3, which incorporated the outcomes and in-puts of European integration, as well as identified the interaction between these elements through 'content' fit/misfit and impacts.

Overall, issues in terms of insurance, pensions, securities and taxation still need to be dealt with. However, since the introduction of the euro and implementation of the FSAP member states have recognized the full importance of a single market in financial services. Indeed, the euro changed the discourse regarding financial services and provided further impetus for compromise and shared beliefs regarding the formulation of a single market in financial services. Through uploading, European integration, downloading and crossloading an integrated market that includes financial services is emerging.

The EU involves a 'process' that is driven by certain ideals relating to 'civil constitution' and 'recognition'. Late 2003 saw Enlargement and the European Constitution. The story is far form over and prediction is difficult. However, informed understanding and the indication of possible directions/paths is not. Theory allows pluralism, which multiplies choice and probable outcomes through limiting dogma. If humanity uses theory to identify the different routes that may be taken then we have a better chance of choosing or developing the most amenable path. Because they can provide images of prospective futures, Kant, Hegel, realism, functionalism, neo-functionalism, intergovernmentalism, multilevel governance, state-centricism and Europeanization all have a role to play in such developments. Different levels of theory with variable degrees of normativism can enable and assist in the formation of different social and political structures. This maybe achieved through utilizing and synthesising methodological approaches.

Notes

1 Recognizing Civil Constitutions: Hegel and Kant as the Basis of Integration Theory?

1. In his categorical imperative Kant argued that duty and obligation should bind humanity. His philosophy is deontological in which the basis of good is a Goodwill. Indeed, the only thing that 'can possibly be conceived in the world … which can be called good without qualification (is) a Goodwill' (Kant, 1987, p. 17). Fundamentally, goodness is not dependent on results but by virtue of it being good. Goodwill is fostered by human beings through acting rationally in accordance with the principles laid down by the categorical imperative. Kant identified the difference between hypothetical and categorical imperatives. Hypothetical imperatives are based on 'if' (if you want to do a do b) such imperatives define what we should do to reach some end. Categorical imperatives do not depend on a particular end, they are ends in themselves they are moral duties. Moral duties are categorical because they should be followed because they are duties and for no other reason. The only answer to the question why should one do their duty? Is because it is one's duty. If another answer existed the imperative would become hypothetical.

   A categorical imperative is one that a fully rational agent would follow. In this context Kant sets up three formulas. First, act only on a maxim or principle that through your will you would have as a universal law of nature. Second, act in such a way as to treat people as means and not ends. Finally, only do something if you are prepared for everyone else to be able to do it as well. According to Kant the highest aspiration of human beings is the development of Goodwill which is developed by acting rationally in accordance with the principles of the categorical imperative.

2. Mutual recognition provides an important mechanism in the pursuit of the Single European Market (SEM) as it allows a framework for compromise. It means recognizing the other in terms of regulatory structures. 'The principle of mutual recognition … pre-supposes agreement on a number of basic rules … these minimum harmonisation requirements … are only possible because common interest, mutual confidence and a high degree of economic convergence exist between EEC member states' (Loheac, 1991, p. 409). The idea behind mutual recognition suggests spontaneous legislative adaptation; however, it does not deal with all regulation and as a convergence point is necessary for it to be effective it could be conceived as an impetus that encourages legislative change and compromise. It provides a basis for acceptance and the rationalization of institutional change.

Mutual recognition may also be considered as a mechanism of crossloading, which is discussed in more detail in Chapter 3.

2 Re-assessing European Integration Theory

1. The dependent variable regarding European integration relates to some sort of end result or outcome. Neither neo-functionalism nor functionalism defined an end result. Neo-functionalism does not draw borders around Europe nor give it a specific form. It is a peaceful process pursuing a peaceful end. However, the material aspect of the end is uncertain. In this context, the limits of European integration are unidentifiable. Indeed, it draws on Kantian political philosophy that identifies a 'just civil constitution', in the abstract but fails to identify it in a concrete form. Furthermore, Enlargement identifies that an end for the EU is difficult to determine while at the same time illustrates aspects of recognition in respect of accession states and applications to join.

3 Uploading, Downloading or Crossloading? Conceptualizing Europeanization and European Integration

1. As noted in the Introduction, this study recognizes that positivism and constructivism may be broken down into more specific methodologies. However, this chapter uses these terms in a general way to identify the differences between scientific approaches, in the context of testing theory through deductive methods, empirical reliability and dependent and independent variables and constructing theory, through empirical validity and inductive and interpretative methods. Furthermore, the chapter recognizes the difference between positivist and post-positivist approaches but again uses positivism in a general context (for further see Lincoln and Guba, 2000 and Guba and Lincoln, 1994).

8 Shared Beliefs and Micro and Macro Uploading

1. Com 91 57 final SYN 329 p. 2.

References

Andersen, S. S. and Eliassen, K. A. (1991) European Community Lobbying. *European Journal of Political Research* 20, 173–87.

Arendt, H. (1989) *Lectures on Kant's Political Philosophy*. University of Chicago Press, Chicago, IL.

Ashead, M. (2002) Conceptualising Europeanization: Policy Networks and Cross-National Comparisons. *Public Policy and Administration Special Issue Understanding the Europeanization of Public Policy* 17(2), 25–42.

BaFIN (2002) *The New Federal Financial Supervisory Authority* (www.bafin.de/english).

Banking Act (1998) Sixth Amendment. Translated by Deutsche Bundesbank and the Federal Financial Supervisory Authority.

Bank of Italy (1999) *Ordinary General Meeting of Shareholders, Abridged Report for the Year 1998*, Rome.

Bank of Italy (2000) *Ordinary General Meeting of Shareholders, Abridged Report for the Year 1999*, Rome.

Bank of Italy (2003) *Ordinary General Meeting of Shareholders, Abridged Report for the Year 2002*, Rome.

Bolkestein, F. (2003) *New EU Member States Still Have Much to Do*. European Affairs, The European Institute, Spring Edition.

Bomberg, E. and Peterson, J. (2000) Policy Transfer and Europeanization: Passing the Heineken Test? *Queens Papers on Europeanization No 2*.

Börzel, T. A. (1999) Institutional Adaptation to Europeanization in Germany and Spain. *Journal of Common Market Studies* 37(4), 573–96.

Börzel, T. A. (2002) Member State Responses to Europeanization. *Journal of Common Market Studies* 40(2), 193–214.

Börzel, T. A. (2003) Shaping and Taking EU Policies: Member State Responses to Europeanization. *Queens Papers on Europeanization No 2*.

Börzel, T. A. and Risse, T. (2000) When Europe Hits Home: Europeanization and Domestic Change. *European Integration Online Papers* 4(15).

Bosco, A. (Ed.) (1991) *The Federal Idea*. Vol. 1. Lothian Foundation Press. UK.

British Insurers International Committee Bulletins (various).

Browne, W. P. (1990) Organized Interests and Their Issue Niches: A Search for Pluralism in a Policy Domain. *Journal of Politics* 52(2) May, 477–509.

Buller, J. and Gamble, A. (2002) Conceptualising Europeanization. *Public Policy and Administration Special Issue Understanding the Europeanization of Public Policy* 17(2), 4–24.

Bulmer, S. and Burch, M. (2001) The Europeanization of Central Government: The UK and Germany in Historical Institutionalist Perspective. In Schneider, G. and Aspinwall, M. (Eds), *The Rules of Integration: Institutional Approaches to the Study of Europe*, pp. 73–98. European Policy Research Unit Series, Manchester University Press, UK.

Caio Koch-Weiser (2002) *German and EU Financial Services*. Presentation at Mansion House, City of London, September.

Calfruny, A. W. and Rosenthal, G. G. (Eds) (1993) *The State of the European Community Vol 2. The Maastricht Debates and Beyond*. Lynne Rienner, Longman.

Camerra-Rowe, P. (1996) *Firms and Collective Representation in the European Union*. The American Political Science Meeting. The San Francisco Hilton and Towers. August 29–September 1. The American Political Science Association.

Canzano, E. C. (1994) Some Strategic Issues in the Insurance Industry Today. *The Geneva Papers on Risk and Insurance* 19(71), April, 127–34.

Carr, E. H. (1993) The Twenty Years Crisis. In Williams, H. Wright, M. and Evans, T. (Eds), *International Relations and Political Theory*, pp. 179–91. Open University Press, Buckingham UK.

Cecchini, P. (1988) *The European Challenge. The Benefits of a Single Market*. Wildwood House, Aldershot.

Cimoszewicz, W. (2002) Poland on the Road to the European Union. Address by Minister of Foreign Affairs of the Republic of Poland at the Nobel Institute Oslo, 8th March.

Cimoszewicz, W. (2002a) Poland on the Threshold of European Membership. Address by Minister of Foreign Affairs of the Republic of Poland at the Hungarian Institute of Foreign Affairs, Budapest 7th February.

Claude, I. L. Jr (1965) *Swords into Ploughshares*. London, UK.

Club De Bruxelles (1994) *Lobbying in Europe After Maastricht*. Club De Bruxelles, Bruxelles.

Coen, D. (1997) The Evolution of the Large Firm as a Political Actor in the European Union. *Journal of European Public Policy* 4(1), March, 91–108.

Coen, D. (1998) European Business Interest and the Nation State: Large Firm Lobbying in the European Union and Member State. *Journal of Public Policy* 18(1), 75–100.

Comité Européen des Assurances (CEA) (1990) *Note on the Proposal for a Third Life Assurance Directive* (October).

Comité Européen des Assurances (CEA) (1990) *Doc. MC 093 09/90*.

Comité Européen des Assurances (CEA) *Position Papers* (various).

Comité Européen des Assurances (CEA) (no date) *Codification of European Insurance Directives*.

Comité Européen des Assurances (CEA INFO) (1994) November and December.

Commission of the European Community (1985) *White Paper on Completing the Internal Market*. Brussels.

Commission of the European Community Report. (1992) *Completing the Internal Market*. European Commission, January.

Cooper, R. (2003) *The Breaking of Nations: Order and Chaos in the Twenty-First Century*. Atlantic Books, UK.

Corbey, D. (1995) Dialectical Functionalism: Stagnation as a Booster of European Integration. *International Organisation* 49(2), Spring, 253–84.

Council and Commission of the European Communities (1992) *Treaty on European Union*. Office for Official Publications of the European Union, Brussels.

Cox, R. W. (1981) Social Forces States and World Orders: Beyond International Relations Theory. *Millenium* 10(2), 126–55.

Cram, L. (1997) *Policy-Making in the European Union. Conceptual Lenses and Integration Processes*. Routledge, London.

Dahrendorf, R. (2003) *The EU Foreign Policy Myth. Financial Times Magazine*, No. 12, July, 23.

Davies, H. (2000) *Untitled*. Eurofi Conference Paris, 15 September.

Davies, H. (2000a) *The Single Financial Market in Five Years Time: How will Regulation Work*. Brussels, 20 March.

Davies, N. (1997) *Europe. A History*. Pimlico, London.

De Gucht, K. (1991) *Report on the Commission's Proposal for a Third Non-Life Directive*. Committee on Legal Affairs and Citizens Rights. Doc EN/ RR/ 112339.

Dehousse, R. (1992) Integration v. Regulation? On the Dynamics of Regulation in the European Community. *Journal of Common Market Studies* 30(4), December, 383–402.

Deutsch, K. W. (1953) *Nationalism and Social Communication*. MIT Press. Cambridge, MA.

Dickinson, G. M. (1990) An Economic Case for the Early Introduction of a Liberal Services Directive for Life Insurance. *Extrait des Annales de Droit de Louvain* Tome L, 1–2.

Directorate-Generale XV. *News From DG XV* (various).

Directorate-Generale XV (1993) *Community Measures in the Field Of Insurance and Pension Funds*. July XV C, 2.

Drabbe, H. (1994) The Internal Market for Insurance: A Reality? *The Geneva Papers on Risk and Insurance* 19(71), April, 135–43.

Dyson, K. (1999) EMU as Europeanization: Convergence, Diversity and Contingency. *Journal of Common Market Studies* 38(4), pp. 645–66.

Dyson, K. (2002) Introduction: EMU as Integration, Europeanization and Convergence. In Dyson, K. (Ed.), *European States and the Euro*. Oxford University Press, UK.

Dyson, K. and Goetz, K. (Draft 11 March 2002), Germany and Europe: Beyond Congruence, presented at Germany and Europe: A Europeanized Germany? Conference, British Academy.

Ellis, T. H. (1990) *European Integration and Insurance. (Creating a Common Insurance Market)*. Witherby and Co., London.

Ellis, T. H. (1995) Policyholder Protection in the Single European Market. In McGee, A. and Heusel, W. (Eds), *The Law and Practice of Insurance in the Single European Market*. Trier Academy of European Law, Germany.

Eltis, W. and Spencer, J. (1993) The Benefits to Europe (and Especially the UK) from Growing Competition and Rapid Expansion in Financial Services. Structural Change in the Service Industry Conference. Cambridge Econometrics, Robinson College Cambridge.

EUR OP (1992) *Treaty on European Union.* Council of the European Communities and Commission of the European Communities. Brussels.

European Commission (1998) *Financial Services: Commission Proposes a Framework for Action* (http://europa.eu.int/).

European Commission (1998a) *Building a Framework for Action,* Com (1998) 625. Brussels.

European Commission (1999) *Financial Services: Commission Outlines Action Plan for Single Financial Market,* 11th May (http://europa.eu.int/).

European Commission (1999a) *Notes of the First Meeting of the Financial Services Policy Group,* 28 January (http://europa.eu.int/).

European Commission (1999b) *Notes of the Second Meeting of the Financial Services Policy Group,* 26 February (http://europa.eu.int/).

European Commission (1999c) *Financial Services Action Plan – First Progress Report,* 29 November (http://europa.eu.int/).

European Commission (2000) *Financial Services: Commission Reports Progress on Action Plan, Outlines New Priorities,* 31 (http://europa.eu.int/).

European Commission (2000a) Financial Services: Commission Calls For Quantum Leep towards Rapid Implementation of Action Plan, 8 November (http://europa.eu.int/).

European Commission (2001). Financial Services: Commission Urges Members States and European Parliament to Deliver on Time, 1 June (http://europa.eu/int/).

European Commission (2002) *Financial Services: Latest Report Highlights Sustained Progress in Integrating EU Capital Markets,* 2 December (http://europa.eu.int/).

European Commission (2002a) *Financial Services Action Plan: Mid-Term Review Emphasises Need for Swift Progress,* 25 February, Brussels.

European Commission (2003) *Financial Services: Latest Report Highlights Need to Boost EU Capital Market Integration in Next Nine Months,* 2 June (http://europa.eu.int/).

European Documentation (1989) *The European Financial Common Market.* Periodical Vol. 4, European Commission, Brussels.

European Parliament (1991) *Europeanisation of the Insurance Industry in the Internal Market After 1992.* Legal Affairs Series W 3 DG for Research.

European Parliament Working Paper (1992) *European Court of Justice (ECJ) Judgement. 4/12/86.*

European Parliament (2001) *The Financial Services Action Plan: Two Years On – Achievements and Prospects.* European Parliamentary Financial Services Forum 15 May, Brussels.

European Parliamentary Financial Services Forum (2001) *The Financial Services Action Plan: Two Years on – Achievements and Prospects.* May, Brussels.

Featherstone, K. and Kazamias, G. (Eds) (2001) *Europeanization and the Southern Periphery.* Frank Cass, London.

Financial Times (1989) 19 May, Editorial.

Financial Times (2003) 15 April, p. 8.

Financial Times Management Report (1992) Insurance in the EC and Switzerland Structure and Development Towards Harmonisation. *Financial Times*, UK.

Fine, L. F. (1997) Recent Developments in EU Insurance Law. *Journal of Insurance Regulation* 16(2), 125.

Fitchew, G. (1988) The View from Brussels. Up-date '88 Conference 1992 – The EEC and Insurance. The Chartered Institute of Insurance.

Fitchew, G. E. (1990) The European Regulatory and Supervisory Framework in Financial Institutions. In Fair, D. E. and Boissien, C. (Eds), *Europe Under New Competitive Conditions*, pp. 27–37 Kluwer, UK.

Foster, N. (1999) *EC Legislation*. Blackstone Press Ltd, London, UK.

Gamble, A. and Kelly, G. (2002) Britain and EMU. In *European States and the Euro: Europeanization, Variation and Convergence*. Dyson, K. (Ed.), Oxford University Press, UK.

Garrett, G. and Tsebelis, G. (1996) An Institutional Critique of Intergovernmentalism. *International Organisation* 50(2), 269–99.

Gehring, T. (1996) Integrating Integration Theory: Neo-functionalism and International Regimes. *Global Society. Journal of Interdisciplinary International Relations* 10(3), 225–54.

George, S. (1976) The Reconciliation of the 'Classical' and 'Scientific' Approaches to International Relations. *Millennium: Journal of International Studies* 5, 28–40.

George, S. (1994) Supranational Actors and Domestic Politics: Integration Theory Reconsidered in the Light of the Single European Act and Maastricht. Sheffield Papers in International Studies No. 22 (University of Sheffield).

George, S. (1995) *Politics and Policy of the European Community*. Oxford University Press, UK.

George, S. (1998) *An Awkward Partner: Britain in the European Community*. Oxford University Press, UK.

George, S. (2001) The Europeanization of UK Politics and Policy-Making: The Effects of European Integration on the UK. UACES/ESRC Workshop Sheffield University, November.

Giulani, M. (2001) Europeanization and Italy: A Bottom-up Process? In Featherstone, K. and Kazamias, G. (Eds), *Europeanization and the Southern Periphery*, pp. 47–72. Frank Cass, London.

Goetz, K. H. and Hix, S. (Eds) (2000) Europeanised Politics? European Integration and National Political Systems. *West European Politics Special Edition* 23(4).

Grant, W. (1995) *Pressure Groups, Politics and Democracy in Britain*. Allen, London.

Greenwood, J. (1995) (Ed.), *European Casebook on Business Alliances. European Casebook Series on Management*. Prentice Hall International, (UK).

Greenwood, J. (1997) *Representing Interests in The European Union*. The European Union Series. Macmillan, London.

Greenwood, J and Cram, L. (1996) European Level Business Collective Action: The Study Agenda Ahead. *Journal of Common Market Studies*. 34(3), 449–63.

Greenwood, J. Grote, J. and Ronit, R. (Eds) (1992) *Organized Interests and the European Community*. Sage, Thousand Oaks, USA.

Guba, E. G. and Lincoln, Y. S. (1994) Competing Paradigms in Qualitative Research. In Denzin, N. and Lincoln, Y. S. (Eds), *Handbook of Qualitative Research*, pp. 105–17. Sage, Thousand Oaks, USA.

Haas, E. B. (1958) *The Uniting of Europe*. Stanford University Press, Stanford, CA.

Haas, E. B. (1964) *Beyond the Nation State. Functionalism and International Organization*. Stanford University Press, Stanford, CA.

Haas, E. B. (1971) The Study of Regional Integration: Reflections on the Joy and Anguish of Pretheorizing. In Lindberg, L. and Scheingold, S. (Eds), *Regional Integration*. Harvard University Press, Cambridge MA.

Haas, E. B. (1975) Is there a Hole in the Whole? Knowledge, Technology, Interdependence and the Construction of International Regimes. *International Organization* 29 (part 3), 827–75.

Haas, E. B. (1976) Turbulent Fields and the Theory of Regional Integration. *International Organization* 30 (part 2), 173–211.

Hampsher-Monk, I. (1995) *A History of Modern Political Thought*. Blackwell Publishers, Oxford.

Hegel, G. W. F. (1967) *Philosophy of Right*. (Trans.) Knox, T. M. Oxford University Press. Clarendon Press, Oxford.

Hegel, G. W. F. (1977) *Phenomenology of Spirit*. (Trans.) Miller, A. V. Foreword Finlay, J. N. Clarendon Press, Oxford.

Hegel, G. W. F. (1988) *Introduction to the Philosophy of History*. (Trans.) Rauch, L. Hackett Publishing, USA.

Heseltine, M. (1992) *Priorities for the UK Presidency*. Association of British Insurers (ABI), Conference 'Target Europe' 15/6.

Hix, S. (1999) *The Political System of the European Union*. Macmillan Press, London.

HMSO (1988) *Treaties Establishing the European Communities*. HMSO, London.

HM Treasury (1997) *UK Membership of the Single Currency: An Assessment of the Five Tests*. HM Treasury, London.

HM Treasury (1999) *Outline National Changeover Plan*. HM Treasury, London.

Hobsbawm, E. (1995) *Age of Extremes. The Short Twentieth Century 1914–1991*. Abacus, London.

Hodges, M. (Ed.) (1972) *European Integration*. Penguin Books, UK.

Hofstede, G. (1995) Insurance as a Product of National Values. *The Geneva Papers on Risk and Insurance* 20(77), October, 423–29.

Hooghe, L. and Marks, G. (1997) Contending Models of Governance in the European Union. In Calfruny, A. W. and Lankowski, C. (Eds), *Europe's Ambitious Unity. Conflict and Consensus in the Post Maastricht Era*. Lynne Reiner, London.

Howell, K. E. (1999) European Union Governance: Sub-National Interests, Supranationality and the Life Insurance Industry. *Current Politics and Economics of Europe* 9(1), 95–115.

Howell, K. E. (2000) *Discovering the Limits of European Integration: Applying Grounded Theory*. Nova Science Books and Journals, New York.

Howell, K. E. (2002) Uploading, Downloading and European Integration: Assessing the Europeanization of UK Financial Services. Paper No. 11, Institute of European Studies Online Journal. Queens University Belfast.

Howell, K. E. (2003) Developing a Conceptualization of Europeanization and European Integration: Mixing Methodologies. ESRC/UACES Seminar Series on the Europeanization of British Public Policy, Paper No. 2. University of Sheffield.

Hurwitz, L. (Ed.) (1980) *Contemporary Perspectives on European Integration.* Aldwych, London.

Insurance Supervision Law (2002 Amendment) Translated by the Federal Financial Supervisory Authority, Bonn.

Kagan, R. (2003) *Power and Paradise. America and Europe in the New World Order.* Atlantic Books, UK.

Kant, I. (1987) *Fundamental Principles of the Metaphysic of Morals.* Prometheus, UK.

Kant, I. (1995) Political Writings (Ed.), Hans Reiss. (Trans.) Nisbet, H. B. *Cambridge Texts in the History of Political Thought.* Cambridge University Press. Cambridge UK.

Kant, I. (1995a) Perpetual Peace a Philosophical Sketch. In Reiss, H. (Ed.), *Political Writings.* Cambridge University Press, UK.

Kant, I. (1995b) Idea for a Universal History with a Cosmopolitan Purpose. In Reiss, H. (Ed.), *Political Writings.* Cambridge University Press, UK.

Keohane, R. and Nye, J. (1977) *Power and Interdependence.* Little Brown and Co., USA.

Keohane, R. and Hoffman, S. (1990) Community Politics and Institutional Change. In Wallace, W. (Ed.), *The Dynamics of European Integration.* The Royal Institute of International Affairs. Pinter, London and New York.

Keohane, R. and Hoffman, S. (1991) Instutional Change in Europe in the 1980s. In *The New European Community: Decision Making and Institutional Change.* Westview, USA.

Kingsdown Inquiry (1995) Action Centre for Europe.

Kirchner, E. J. (1976) *An Empirical Examination of the Functionalist Concept of Spillover.* Case Western Reserve University, USA.

Kirchner, E. J. (1980) Interest Group Behaviour at Community Level. In Hurwitz, L. (Ed.), *Contemporay Perspectives on European Integration.* Aldwych, London.

Kirchner, E. J. (1992) *Decision-Making in the European Community: The Council Presidency and European integration.* Manchester University Press, UK.

Kirchner, E. J. and Schwaiger, H. (1981) *The Role of Interest Groups in the European Community.* Economic and Social Committee of the EC. Gower, Aldershot, UK.

Kojeve, A. (1980) *Introduction to the Reading of Hegel: Lectures on the Phenomenology of Spirit.* Cornell University Press, USA.

Komorowski, S. (2003) *Poland – a Partner and Ally in Europe.* European Culture Society, Kings College London, 6 March.

Ladrech, R. (1994) Europeanization of Domestic Politics and Institutions: The Case of France. *Journal of Common Market Studies* 32(1), 69–87.

Lieber, R. J. (1974) Interest Groups and Political Integration in British entry into Europe. In Kimber, A. and Richardson, J. J. (Eds), *Pressure Groups in Britain*, pp. 27–56. Dent Publishers, London.

Lincoln, Y. S. and Guba, E. G. (2000) Paradigmatic Controversies, Contradictions and Emerging Confluences. In Denzin, N. K. and Lincoln, Y. S. (Eds), *Handbook of Qualitative Research*. Sage, Thousand Oaks, USA.

Lindberg, L. N. (1963) The *Political Dynamics of European Integration*. Stanford University Press, USA.

Lindberg, L. (1967) The European Community as a Political System: Notes Toward the Construction of a Model. *Journal of Common Market Studies* 5(4), June, 344–87.

Lindberg, L. and Scheingold, S. A. (1970) *Europe's Would-Be Polity: Patterns of Change in the European Community*. Prentice Hall, Englewood Cliffs, NJ.

Linn, J. F. (2001) *Progresses and Challenges in Financial Sector Developments for Poland and Other Advanced Transition Economies in the Process of EU-Integration*. The World Bank, June.

Linter, V. and Mazey, S. (1991) *The European Community: Economic and Political Aspects*. McGraw Hill, London.

Loheac, F. (1991) Deregulation of Financial Services and Liberalization of International Trade in Services. *The Geneva Papers on Risk and Insurance Issues and Practice*. No. 61, October, 406–13.

Loheac, F. (1992) *Wider EC Issues*. ABI Conference 'Target Europe' 15 June Association of British Insurers, UK.

Marks, G. (1993) Structural Policy and Multilevel Governance. In Calfruny, A. W. and Rosenthal, G. G. (Eds), *The State of the European Community. The Maastrcht Debate and Beyond Vol 2*. Lynne Rienner, Longman.

Marks, G., Scharpf, F. W. Schmitter, P. C. and Streeck, W. (Eds) (1996) *Governance in the European Union*. Sage, Thousand Oaks, USA.

Marks, G., Hooghe, L. and Blank, K. (1996a) European Integration from the 1980s: State-Centric v. Multi-level Governance. *Journal of Common Market Studies* 34(3), 341–78.

Mazey, S. P. and Richardson, J. J. (1993) Interest Groups in the European Community. In Richardson J. J. (Ed.), *Pressure Groups*. Oxford University Press.

Mazey, S. P. and Richardson, J. J. (1996) *The Logic of Organisation. Interest Groups*. In Richardson, J. J. (Ed.), *European Union Power and Policy-Making*. Routledge, London.

McGee, A. and Heusel, W. (Eds) (1995) *The Law and Practice of Insurance in the Single Market*. The Trier Academy of European Law Vol. 11.

McKay, D. (2002) The Political Economy of Fiscal Policy under Monetary Union. In Dyson, K. (Ed.), *European States and the Euro: Europeanization, Variation and Convergence*. Oxford University Press, USA.

McLaughlin, A. M. (1995) Automobiles: Dynamic Orgainisations in Turbulent Times? In Greenwood, J. (Ed.), *European Casebook on Business Alliances*, pp. 172–83. Prentice Hall International, UK.

McLaughlin, A. M. and Greenwood, J. (1995) The Management of Interest Representation in the European Union. *Journal of Common Market Studies* 33(1), March, 143–6.

McLaughlin, A. M, Jordan, G. and Maloney, W. A. (1993) Corporate Lobbying in the European Community. *Journal of Common Market Studies* 31(2), June, 192–213.

Mitrany, D. A (1943) *Working Peace System*. Royal Institute of International Affairs, London.

Mitrany, D. A. (1944) *The Road to Security*. Peace News Pamphlet No. 29, London, NPC.

Mitrany, D. A. (1965) The Prospect of Integration Federal or Functional. *Journal of Common Market Studies* 4, December, 119–49.

Mitrany, D. A. (1970) The Functional Approach to World Organization. In Cosgrave, C. A. and Twitchett, K. (Eds), *New International Actors: The United Nations and the EEC*, pp. 65–75. Macmillan, London.

Mitrany, D. A. (1975a) A Political Theory for a New Society. In Groom, P. and Taylor, A. (Eds), *Functionalism* University of London Press, London UK.

Mitrany, D. A. (1975b) Functionalism: Theory and Practice in International Relations. In Groom, P. and Taylor, A. (Eds), *Functionalism*. University of London Press, London UK.

Mitrany, D. A. (1975c) *The Functional Theory of Politics*. London School of Economics Press, London.

Moe, T. M. (1980) *The Organisation of Interests*. University of Chicago Press, Chicago and London.

Moravcsik, A. (1991) Negotiating the Single European Act. In Keohane, R. and Hoffman, S. (Eds), *The New European Community: Decision-Making and Institutional Change*. Westview Publishers, USA.

Moravcsik, A. (1993) Preferences and Power in the European Community: A liberal Intergovernmentalist Approach. *Journal of Common Market Studies* 31, 473–524.

Moravcsik, A. (1998) *The Choice for Europe*. Cornell University Press, USA.

Morgenthau, H. J. (1973) *Politics Among Nations. The Struggle for Power and Peace*. Alfred Knope, New York.

Munich Re (1992) *Life Insurance in the EC and EFTA Countries*. Eurofolder.

Munich Re (1988) *A Series of Notes on Insurance in the EC*. Munich Re.

Mutimer, D. (1989) 1992 and the Political Integration of Europe: Neo-functionalism Reconsidered. *Journal of European Integration* XIII(1), 75–101.

Nugent, N. (1999) *The Government and Politics of the European Union*. Macmillan, UK.

Nye, J. S. (1971) Comparing Common Markets: A Revised Neo-Functionalist Model. In Lindberg, L. and Scheigold, S. A. (Eds), *Regional Integration: Theory and Research*. Harvard University Press, Cambridge, MA.

Nye, J. S. (1971a) *Peace in Parts. Integration and Conflict in Regional Organisation*. Little Brown and Company, Harvard, USA.

Observer Newspaper (2003) *Euro Will pay for NHS, Says Blair*. 20 July, p. 11.

Official Journals of the European Community (various).

Official Journal of the European Community. (1993) *An Open and Structured Dialogue Between the Commission and Interest Groups* (OJ 93/C63).

O'Leary, A. (1988) *Freedom of Services, Life Insurance*. Up-date '88 Conference 1992 – The EEC & Insurance. The Chartered Institute of Insurers. London UK

Olsen, J. P. (2002) *The Many Faces of Europeanization*. Arena Working Papers 01/02.

Olson, M. (1993) The Logic of Collective Action. In Richardson, J. J. (Ed.), *Pressure Groups*. Oxford University Press.

Palliser, M. Rt Hon. (1992) *Investment and Finance – Issues for the Single Market*. ABI Conference 'Target Europe' 15/6, ABI, London UK.

Parkinson, F. (1977) *The Philosophy of International Relations: A Study in Political Thought*. Sage Library of Social Research 52.

Pedersen, T. (1992) Political Change in the European Community. The Single European Act as a Case of System Transformation. *Co-operation and Conflict* 27(part 1), 7–44.

Pentland, C. (1975) Functionalism and Theories of International Political Integration. In Groom, P. and Taylor, A. (Eds), *Functionalism*. University of London, UK.

Petersen, J. (1995) Decision-making in the European Union: Towards a Framework for Analysis. *Journal of European Public Policy* 2(1), March, 69–93.

Pierson, P. (1996) The Path to European Integration: A Historical Institutionalist Analysis. *Comparative Political Studies* 29(2), April, 123–63.

Pinder, J. (1993) The Single Market: A Step Toward Union. In Lodge, J. (Ed.), *The European Community and the Challenge of the Future*, pp. 51–68. Pinter, London.

Pippin, R. B. (1997) *Idealism as Modernism*. Cambridge University Press, UK.

Polish Securities and Exchange Commission (1998) *The Most Important Events in 1998*, Section Eight, Annual Report.

Pool, W. E. (1990) *The Creation of the Internal Market in Insurance. Commission of the European Communities*. The Commission of the European Communities Document, Brussels.

Pool, W. E. (1992). Insurance and the European Community. *The Geneva Papers on Risk and Insurance Issues and Practice* No. 63, April, 338–402.

Popper, K. R. (1994) *The Myth of the Framework. In Defence of Science and Rationality*. Routledge, London.

Popper, K. R. (2002) *The Logic of Scientific Discovery*. Routledge Classics, London and New York.

Puchala, D. (1972) Of Blind Men, Elephants and International Integration. *Journal of Common Market Studies* 12(2), 267–84.

Radaelli, C. M. (2000) Whither Europeanization? Concept Stretching and Substantive Change. *European Integration Online Papers* (EIoP) Vol. 4.

Randone, E. (1990) Third Geneva Lecture. The International Strategy of European Insurance Companies. *The Geneva Papers on Risk and Insurance* 15(57), October, 364–71.

Randzio-Plath, C. (2001) Introduction-Speech. Conference Euro 2002: The Consequences for the Real Economy – the Euro and Brussels. Budapest 13/14 September, European Parliament.

Rees, N. A. G. (1992). The Politics or Regional Development in the European Community: An Inter-Organisational Perspective. PhD, University of South Carolina, USA.

Richardson, J. J. (Ed.) (1996) *European Union. Power and Policy-Making.* European Public Policy. Routledge, London UK.

Richardson, J. J. (1996a) Policy-Making in the EU. Interests, Ideas and Garbage Cans of Primeval Soup. In Richardson, J. J. (Ed.), *European Union. Power and Policy-Making.* European Public Policy. Routledge, London UK.

Ringmar, E. (1995) The Relevance of International Law: A Hegelian Interpretation of a Peculiar 17th century Pre-occupation. *Review of International Studies* 21, 87–103.

Risse, T., Green Cowles, M. and Corporosa, J. (2001) *Europeanization and Domestic Change Introduction in Europeanization and Domestic Change: Pages 1–20 Transforming Europe.* Cornell University Press, Ithaca NY.

Russell, A. (1988) *The UK Supervisor's View.* Up-date '88 Conference 1992 – The EEC & Insurance.

Sandholtz, W. (1994) Choosing Union: Monetary Politics and Maastricht. In Neilsen, B. F. and Stubb, A. C.-G. (Eds), *The European Union. Readings on the Theory and Practice of European Integration.* Lynne Rienner, London.

Sandholtz, W. and Zysman, J. (1989) 1992: Recasting the European bargain. *World Politics* 42, 95–129.

Scheingold, S. (1971) Domestic and International Consequences of Regional Integration. In Lindgerg, L. and Scheingold, S. A. (Eds), *Regional Integration: Theory and Research.* Harvard University Press, Cambridge, MA.

Schmidt, R. (1989). The First Geneva Lecture. The Practical Consequences for Insurers of the Freedom of Services throughout the European Community. The Geneva Papers on Risk and Insurance Supplement No. 51, April.

Schmitter, P. C. (1971) A Revised Theory of Regional Integration. In Lindgerg, L. and Scheingold, S. A. (Eds), *Regional Integration: Theory and Research.* Harvard University Press, Cambridge, MA.

Schmitter, P. C. (1996) Examining the Present Euro-Polity with the Help of Past Theories. In Marks, G., Scharpf, F. W., Schmitter, P. C. and Streeck, W. (Eds), *Governance in the European Union.* Sage, Thousand Oaks, USA.

Schneider, V. *et al.* (1994) Corporate Actors Networks in European Policy-Making: Harmonizing Telecommunication Policy. *Journal of Common Market Studies* 32(4), 473–98.

Sewell, J. P. (1966) *Functionalism and World Politics.* Princeton University Press, USA.

Shapiro, S. (1997) Open EU Market Still in the Works. *Business Insurance* 31(2), 23–6.

Sidjanski, D. (1970) Pressure Groups and the EEC. In Cosgrave and Twitchett (Eds), *New International Actors: The United Nations and the EEC*, pp. 222–36. Macmillan, London.

Stirk, M. R. and Weigal, D. (1999) *The Origins and Development of European Integration.* Pinter, London and New York.

Swiss Re (UK) (1989) *Sigma* no 2.

Swiss Re (UK) (1990) *Sigma* no 1.

Swiss Re (UK) (1990) *Sigma* no 4.

Swiss Re (UK) (1991) *Sigma* no 2.

Swiss Re (UK) (1992) *Sigma* no 1.

Taylor, P. (1968) The Functionalist Approach to the Problem of International Order. *Political Studies*, October, 393–410.

Taylor, P. (1980) Interdependence and Autonomy in the European Communities: The Case of the European Monetary System. *Journal of Common Market Studies* XVIII(4), June, 370–87.

Third Life Insurance Directive (1992) the Coordination of Laws, Regulations and Administrative Provisions Relating to Direct Life Assurance 92/96/EEC, amending Directives 79/267/EEC and 90/619/EEC.

Tranholme-Mikkelson, J. (1991) Neo-functionalism Obstinate v Obsolete. *Millenium: Journal of International Studies* 20, 1–22.

Ugur, M. (1997) State-Society Interaction and European Integration: A Political Economy Approach to the Dynamics of Policy-Making of the European Union. *Review of International Studies* 23, 469–500.

Vipond, P. (1995) European Banking and Insurance. Business Alliances and Corporate Strategies. In Greenwood, J. (Ed.), *European Casebook on Business Alliances*. Prentice Hall, UK.

Wallace, H. (1990) Making Multilateral Negotiations Work. In Wallace, W. (Ed.), *The Dynamics of European Union*. Royal Institute of International Affairs, Pinter, London.

Walsh, W. H. (1969) *Hegelian Ethics*. Thoemmes Press, USA.

Ward, K. (1972) *The Development of Kant's View of Ethics*. Blackwell Publishers, Oxford.

Webb, C. (1983) Theoretical Perspectives and Problems in Policy Making. In Wallace, W., Wallace, H. and Webb, C. (Eds), *The European Community*. John Wiley & Son, London.

Williams, H., Moorhead, W. and Evans, T. (1993) *International Relations and Political Theory*. Open University Press, Buckingham, UK.

Index